MILLION DOLLAR CONSULTING PROPOSALS

How to Write a Proposal That's Accepted Every Time

ALAN WEISS

WILEY

JOHN WILEY & SONS, INC.

Library of Congress Cataloging-in-Publication Data:

Weiss, Alan, 1946–
    Million dollar consulting proposals : how to write a proposal that's accepted every time/Alan Weiss.—1
        p. cm.
    Includes index.
    ISBN 978-1-118-09753-3 (pbk.); ISBN 978-1-118-15000-9 (ebk);
    ISBN 978-1-118-15001-6 (ebk); ISBN 978-1-118-15002-3 (ebk)
        1. Business consultants. 2. Consulting firms—Management. 3. Consultants—Marketing.
    I. Title.
    HD69.C6.W4598 2011
    001—dc23

                                                    2011022699

This book is dedicated to Koufax, the Wonder Dog, and Buddy Beagle, both of whom create irresistible proposals.

Contents

Chapter 7

Chapter 8

Chapter 9

Chapter 10

In the Unlikely Event You Need Oxygen: We Don't Anticipate a Crash, But There Are Some Things You Ought to Know   171

Acknowledgments

I'd like to thank Shannon Vargo and the editors at John Wiley & Sons for their constant support and collegiality over the years. My thanks also to superagent Jeff Herman.

I've had several careers, often concurrently. I've consulted with Fortune 1000 organizations globally; delivered keynote speeches before large audiences; written more than 40 books; become a consultant to consultants as a mentor and coach; and formed worldwide communities of entrepreneurs. Throughout those experiences one issue arose, which was equivalent to a synapse in the brain, passing electrical signals: the critical nature of the proposal that spanned the conceptual agreement and the relationship with the buyer, *and* the formal agreement to proceed with stipulated fees and their payment terms.

Unlike those instantaneous brain waves, however, I found that many entrepreneurs' proposals created not linkages but blockages, and they created movement only slightly slower than a receding glacier.

We've all seen the "coffee table" proposals, with 30 pages of résumés ("John enjoys fly-fishing"), 20 pages of credibility ("Winner of the Greater Tacoma Not Shrinking Company Award, Honorable Mention"), and 10 pages of nonsensical flowcharts and graphs that look like the innards of the Hubble Telescope. On the other extreme are those who boast of a "handshake proposal," which holds up nicely until the buyer leaves, the conditions change, or the memories grow short.

In this book (which is the modern iteration of my classic *How to Write a Proposal That's Accepted Every Time*, first written in 2002, which sold for $149), you'll learn how to write a proposal in about 45 minutes that is 2.5 pages long, no matter how big the project. The proposal will incorporate subtle features providing for an 80 percent or better success rate, and with maximum protection for you. You'll avoid legal departments, maximize your fees, and create a passionate commitment on the part of your client.

Sound useful?

People who have taken this approach have sent me all kinds of positive examples and accolades, and the average income in additional fees the first six months of using it is $40,000. Just a month before writing this introduction I helped a technology consultant raise his highest options from $77,000 to $377,000, which was accepted by his client with 50 percent paid on acceptance.

And that's not unusual.

We've been able to completely recast this book (it's 75 percent different) from its predecessor; provide an online, evolving appendix; and lower the price by more than $100! That's because John Wiley & Sons and I have a long and happy history together, and the editors and I believe this book can change lives.

Please proceed with an open mind. What I've created may seem extremely simple. There's a good reason for that perception.

It is.

—Alan Weiss, PhD
East Greenwich, RI
June 2011

Business Vows

What Is a Proposal and Why It Is Necessary

What They Can Do and What They Can't Do

A proposal is a summation, not an explanation. It is a summary of the conceptual agreement you've reached with an economic buyer and not a negotiating document or an attempt to make a sale.

Therefore, it is formed only *after* conceptual agreement with the buyer has been completed. We talk more about this later in the chapter, but at the outset it's important to understand that I'm not talking about the generic or stereotypical proposal in this book. Proposals are a summary of what's come before, to which the buyer has already agreed, and constitute the connection (the synapse from the introduction of this book) to the launch of the project. Proposals are organic documents, which are used to guide and monitor the project, and are not immediately archaic fossils of the Pleistocene Epoch intended for dusty display cases and remote shelves.

1

Here is what an outstanding proposal can do:

- Summarize and convey formally the conceptual agreements reached in discussions to that point between you and the economic buyer.
- Detail the objectives of the project.
- Provide for the metrics of success.
- Describe the value that will occur once the objectives are met (both personally and professionally).
- Supply options from which the buyer can choose to determine the amount of value sought in return on the investment (ROI) committed.
- Stipulate fees, expense reimbursement, and payment terms.
- Enable immediate acceptance in writing.

My proposals serve as the contract as well as the offer of the contract. They are in plain English, without "third parties shall hold harmless," because if you include boilerplate legalese, you will ensure that the proposal will wind up in the hands of your prospect's lawyers, who are so conservative and protective that they'd prefer that the firm not even open the doors every morning in order to prevent any harm from befalling the enterprise.

Here is what proposals cannot and should not do:

- Enable a nonbuyer (gatekeeper, HR, or training person) to proceed to a buyer on your behalf.
- Establish your credibility.
- Establish a relationship with a buyer.
- Serve as a point of comparison for competitors' proposals.
- Offer vague promises or results and outcomes.

Case Study: The Federal Reserve

I had submitted my normal 2.5-page proposal to the Fed in New York, the largest of the Federal Reserve Banks. I had been recommended by some of the banks they supervise, which were clients of mine.

It was mandatory to allow legal to review all proposals, and they took two precious weeks, returning a 32-page monstrosity. Once my buyer and I read it—a painful undertaking—we were shocked to find virtually no difference whatsoever, no changes in my aggressive fees or payment terms, but instead an additional 29.5 pages of language worthy of the Rosetta Stone to interpret.

Lawyers are hopeless at two pursuits: running a professional firm based on value, and using the English language to convey meaning.

- Include agreements that the buyer has not agreed to prior.
- Serve as a "take it or leave it" alternative.
- Cite legal provisions and covenants.
- Be valid and acceptable without time limits.
- Serve as an agreement for nonvalue relationships, such as pricing by day, participant, materials, labor, and so forth.[1]

What I'm telling you—and what will influence this entire book—is that proposals have traditionally been viewed incorrectly in professional services. They have been a gallimaufry of credibility, research, consultant's beliefs and mission, pricing, risk management, and competitive submission.

> ### Glossary
>
> *Economic buyer:* That individual who can produce a check in return for the value expressed in your proposal without any other approvals from anyone else.
>
> *Conceptual agreement:* Concurrence with that buyer about the objectives for the project, the metrics that will measure progress and/or success, and the value to the organization and the buyer that will accrue as a result of meeting those objectives.
>
> *Gatekeeper:* Any person who cannot say yes but can say no and sees it as his or her responsibility to keep you distant from the buyer. In most cases this will include the entire human resources, training, and/or learning and development areas.

All of that is wrong. Those issues need to be covered prior to the proposal being created.

I had been consulting with a pharmaceutical consulting firm in New York for a couple of years, right through a lucrative sale to a larger operation. The most important thing I accomplished was to persuade the firm to stop using a metric of "number of proposals issued per week"! Supposedly, this number was an indicator of sales success (e.g., "27 firms asked for our proposals") but the "hit rate" was dreadful and an entire back office of resources was wasted creating huge, assembly-line proposals.

Proposals are not the point of the arrow, they are the heft behind the arrow. The penetration and aerodynamics are based on other factors, and we turn to those now to put the positioning and creation of proposals in perspective.

Ironically, most people submit proposals far too early and far too often. They are actually at the conclusion of the sales process, just prior to a project's launch. When a proposal is accepted, you should be able to begin work immediately.

Their Place in Your Business Model

If you don't know what your business model is, then you have more problems than merely creating better proposals! A relationship with a client is a series of small yeses that culminate in a signed agreement—a proposal that's accepted. Figure 1.1 is an example of a simple but highly effective business model:

You begin with a common value system. I don't mean a spiritual or religious belief system, but an agreement about business.

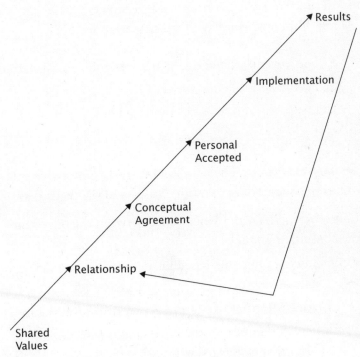

FIGURE 1.1 A consulting business model

For example, I've never performed downsizing or "rightsizing" (now *there's* a euphemism) because I believe that such actions are simply an attempt to atone for mistakes made in the executive suite. Getting rid of one or two executives who made poor decisions is far better than dumping hundreds of people who have been trying their best. (And experience shows that more than 90 percent of attempts to severely restrict costs and improve profits in downsizing fail to reach their goals.)

That's what I mean by shared values. If those are in place, you develop a trusting relationship with the buyer. This must be the economic buyer we spoke of earlier. That relationship may take 30 minutes or three meetings. (If it takes several months and you still haven't achieved it, assume that you two just weren't meant for each other.) That trusting relationship is essential in my model in order to ensure conceptual agreement.

How you know you have a trusting relationship:

- The buyer shares personal and nonpublic information.
- The buyer asks your advice.

Glossary

Trusting relationship: The buyer and you are comfortable volunteering, questioning, "pushing back," and sharing issues.

Conceptual agreement: Concurrence between the buyer and the consultant about:

Objectives: Outcome-based business results, not deliverables or tasks.

Metrics: Measures of progress, success, and/or finality.

Value: The impact on the buyer and organization in meeting the objectives.

- You and the buyer challenge each other's assumptions.
- You feel free to interrupt each other without ill feelings.
- The buyer does not allow interruptions when with you.
- The buyer admits to uncertainty or a welcome new view from you.

The purpose of the trusting relationship is to ensure that the buyer is honest about the next step—the conceptual agreement. This is where you and the buyer jointly frame objectives, metrics, and value.[2]

An objective is a business result, never a "deliverable" (a favorite word of nonbuyers, primarily in the human resources department). When someone presents you with an input, turn it into an output by asking, "Why is that important?"

Examples:

- Deliverable: Strategy retreat.
  - Outcome: New strategy to penetrate overseas markets.
- Deliverable: Coaching for senior vice president.
  - Outcome: Improved presence with media to improve company reputation.
- Deliverable: Focus groups.
  - Output: Gain customer contributions for best features that will improve sales in product reinvention.

A metric is an observable, detectable indicator of progress or final success.

Examples from above:

- Deliverable: Strategy retreat.
  - Outcome: New strategy to penetrate overseas markets.

- Metric: All P&L leaders create support for strategy within two weeks.
- Deliverable: Coaching for senior vice president.
  - Outcome: Improved presence with media to improve company reputation.
  - Metric: More positive articles appear in trade press resulting from his appearances.
- Deliverable: Focus groups.
  - Output: Gain customer contributions for best features that will improve sales in product reinvention.
  - Metric: Five innovative ideas that both R&D and sales support with their budgets.

Finally, value is the impact of meeting the objective. It may sometimes be the same, because increased profit is an objective and it can also be considered as the value. But there is additional value from increased profit, such as the ability to reinvest in the business, pay higher dividends, pay down debt, improve credit rating, and so on.

Examples from above:

- Deliverable: Strategy retreat.
  - Outcome: New strategy to penetrate overseas markets.
  - Metric: All P&L leaders create support for strategy within two weeks.
  - Value: Global presence will improve profit, diversify exposure to volatile markets, and attract new labor pools.
- Deliverable: Coaching for senior vice president.
  - Outcome: Improved presence with media to improve company reputation.

- Metric: More positive articles appear in trade press resulting from his appearances.
- Value: Attract more talented candidates for key positions with less cost of acquisition.
- Deliverable: Focus groups.
  - Output: Gain customer contributions for best features that will improve sales in product reinvention.
  - Metric: Five innovative ideas that both R&D and sales support with their budgets.
  - Value: Early adapters will provide immediate boost and momentum for new product introductions, which will be fully supported by our two key departments.

Only at this point, after conceptual agreement, do we create a proposal that is a summation of that agreement (and with options and peripheral information that we cover a bit later). That proposal enables a partnership to be consummated, a project delivered, *and results generated that reinforce the relationship, creating the potential for additional business in the present and referral business for the future.*[3]

Why You Don't Provide Proposals for Just Anyone

A proposal with the wrong input and in the wrong hands is a ticking bomb waiting to blast you right out of the prospect. Don't fall into the trap of thinking that a request for a proposal is a green light and an open door. You may just be smashing into a wall.

Here's why anyone beneath the true, economic buyer cannot contribute to your proposal:

- They are generally unfamiliar with organizational strategy, do not have a broad view, and take a very narrow position.

- They will default to tasks, inputs, and deliverables. They do not tend to think in terms of outcome and results, where the real value for the project (and your fees) actually resides.

- They think small. They don't think globally or innovatively.

- They are afraid of being critiqued and tend to be highly conservative instead of prudent risk takers; they are risk averse.

- They will eschew accepting or assigning any kind of internal accountability because they are scared or they simply can't.

Here's why you can't submit a proposal, no matter if you actually obtained quality input somehow, to anyone less than a true buyer:

- They will not have your passion to represent it and evangelize about it.

- They will tend to see it as a negotiating position once any others raise any type of resistance.

- They have no authority to move ahead in any case, and are simply middle people.

- Their priorities will tend not to include the project and they will sacrifice it if there is resistance from superiors.

- They will not be able to answer even reasonable questions about implementation.

I could go on, but I think you get my drift. You're better off with no proposal than with a good proposal in the wrong hands. We talk in Chapter 3 specifically about how to identify, avoid, and mitigate the effects of gatekeepers, but for this overview let's establish that you *cannot* provide them with proposals.

If you believe and buy into my position that proposals should be summations of conceptual agreement and not explorations of "fit" and acceptability of work, then it shouldn't be a great leap to understand why nonbuyers can't be recipients of proposals.

Occasionally, there is a key recommender who *can* get you to a buyer, but even that person should be used to create the beginning of a relationship, preproposal, and not be the channel through which the proposal is launched. I've had the good fortune to work with a half-dozen (they are that rare) key recommenders over the years, people who are completely trusted by line buyers. They have positioned me in front of the right people at the right time. But I've never asked one to provide input for or be the purveyor of the proposal itself.

That is between me and the buyer.

You also have to be careful that your proposal is not used as a competitive calibration. I've seen some prospects—especially people at low levels in those prospects who are accustomed to dealing with "vendors"—use the proposals to try to gain lower fees or better features from competing firms. You should place a copyright on your client proposals, and include these lines: "This proposal is intended solely for Adam Avery, senior vice president of Acme Rockets, and is for the exclusive purpose of creating a partnership between Acme and Summit for the project described herein. It may not be distributed or shared with others without our express approval."

That may sound harsh, but a proposal is your intellectual property and not attempting to prevent others from seeing it is like leaving the back door open, the light on, and the combination to the safe taped to the window. You're asking to be robbed.

Most organizations have an assortment of what I call "feasibility buyers." They can't sign a check, can say no but not yes, and may actually advise the buyer. They may constitute expertise in matters financial, cultural, technical, sales, research, politics, and/or simply be a trusted sounding board. That's why you need your own direct relationship with the buyer, and not merely with those jockeying for position in the buyer's favor. I know how harsh this may sound, but it's the difference between placing the right bet on a favored horse and placing a bet on a losing horse whose race was already run.

Proposals aren't business cards. Don't hand them out to just anyone who wants one as if you have an unlimited supply.

The Role of Conceptual Agreement

Ironically, the longer one takes to gain a trusting relationship, the more quickly proposals for major projects are accepted. That sounds counterintuitive, but it's true.

Conceptual agreement is concurrence in theory about what will take place. Once you create this with a true buyer, the proposal will merely support and substantiate that agreement. You want to leave as little as possible open to confusion, resistance, and uncertainty.

In the model presented in Figure 1.1, you can understand why the trusting relationship must precede conceptual agreement (and why a logical and sequential business model is so important to create). The buyer is not going to share the components of conceptual agreement (and, therefore, your eventual proposal) without trust.

There are four basic objections you're going to encounter as you progress in this model, and three of them are specious:

1. No money

    There is always money! The lights are on, the floors are clean, people at their desks are being paid. Professional services providers think that money is a *resource.* It is not. It's a *priority.* So the question is really not one of finding money but of moving money that already exists from something else to you.

2. No time.

We tend to immediately agree that "timing is tough" or "there's a better time" and agree to wait six months for an answer (which never comes). But time, too, is not a scarce resource, because we know that every day we have 24 hours. The question is how we invest it for ourselves and for others we direct. Therefore, time is also not a resource, *but a priority.* Are you important enough in terms of your value to demand a portion of existing time?

3. No need.

In this case the buyer doesn't see a need, which is almost impossible, because it's your job to *create need.* You do that by asking "Why?," or by identifying existing need (e.g., competitive inroads), or by creating need (e.g., marketing traditional services electronically), or by anticipating need (shouldn't you be making plans about the China market?). Your value distance, Figure 1.2, is your ability to listen to what the prospect wants and find the true, far more valuable, needs.

4. No trust.

This is the only valid area of resistance, and the preceding three are only subterfuges used to mask this one (which is more difficult to raise and talk about honestly, and is often subliminal in any case). If I don't trust you—that is, I haven't been convinced of your credibility, integrity, and quality—then all the other excuses take on artificial heft.

This is why conceptual agreement based on trust is so vital. I've had buyers say to me, "I've received so much value from this

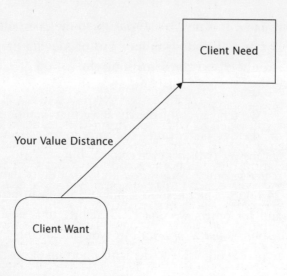

FIGURE 1.2 Value distance

conversation that I'm not sure how we can use you yet, but I want to pursue something with you because we need you around here!" That's an invitation to write your own ticket.

Conceptual agreement on the objectives (outcomes), metrics (measures of progress and success), and value (impact on the organization and the buyer) are the heart and soul of the proposal. You need to work on these for as long as required, but also learn to accelerate that process. Once the buyer is nodding in assent as he or she reads the details of the proposal, the buyer is far more likely to accept the "new" elements: options, fees, and terms.

The Concept of Value (Not Time and Materials)

The proposal philosophy, examples, and techniques you'll find in subsequent pages are all based on the premise that you and I work for a fee based on value, not time, materials, numbers of participants, or other commodity determinations. It's worth taking a few minutes here to dwell on this considerable distinction.

The value of your collaboration with a client is based on the contribution you make to improving the client's condition. The buyer and you agree to what you deem that to be in the conceptual agreement aspect of the proposal. Having established a trusting relationship, you both intend to partner to each reasonable objective with conservative value attached. (The questions for ensuring this appear in the next chapter.)

I have heard consulting "experts" claim that the formula for fees should be your monetary needs divided by the hours you have available to consult, providing you with an hourly rate. There are only 600 things gravely mistaken about this notion, but here are the most important:

- No one wants to work the maximum hours available in a business that demands physical presence and commensurate travel.

- Your presence is *not* your value in any case, because it's often irrelevant to the results (the objectives).

- Pricing by participant, time unit, or materials provided is a commodity mind-set that invites comparison to others, and you will never be the low-price provider (or at least not be the low-price provider and establish any kind of decent lifestyle).

- Wealth is discretionary time, so the idea is to maximize discretionary time through nonlabor intensive work, which is antithetical to hourly or daily fees.

- Your strategy should be one of markets served or services offered, but not production capability, as if you were a steel mill or a paper plant. The huge monolithic consulting firms such as McKinsey and Deloitte are production-capability driven, meaning that they're paying people $350 an hour and must bill them out at $550 an hour to make a profit. That's why the "Big 8" of years ago is today about a "Big 3.5" and diminishing. It's an antediluvian business model.

- The client is best served (remember about "improving the client's condition") by a fast improvement or resolution, not a slow one. But time-based billing rewards sloth and lethargy. Billing by the hour or day is intrinsically unethical. That's right, I said it: *unethical.* Lawyers traditionally bill by six-minute intervals, and we all know how much we trust lawyers.[4]

- You don't want the client to have to make an investment decision every time your help may be needed, nor do you want to be seen as self-aggrandizing if you realize that you need to put in more time.

- Your value is in your advice, not your presence. Otherwise, why would anyone pay for a retainer, which is the ultimate relationship with a client. (Of no small irony is the fact that a lawyer's "retainer" is nothing more than a deposit against subsequent six-minute billing totals.)

I'll skip the other 592 reasons out of respect for your time and the length of this book, but I think you get the idea.

The value distance in Figure 1.2 shows how much we can demonstrate value when we adapt this approach. The worst position for a consultant is to be seen as a commodity, readily comparable to others.

This is why your initial approach to all prospects must be with a value-based mentality. That may take some reeducating

---

Glossary

Value-based fees are the remuneration you receive as your contribution to the value derived by the client as a result of meeting agreed-upon business results (objectives). They provide a dramatic return on investment for the client and equitable compensation for the consultant.

---

on your part with buyers, because they've been miseducated by countless consultants before you. But if you use the bullet points on the previous pages, this is easily accomplished. Here is the standard language I use when asked about my fee "basis":

> *My fee is based on my contribution to the value we have agreed should result from this project, representing a dramatic return on investment for you and equitable compensation for me.*

What is "equitable compensation"? It's based on that dramatic return. I've found that if you can provide a 10:1 return *with the involvement of the buyer in conceptual agreement about objectives, measures, and value,* the client is overjoyed. (Where else is the client getting that kind of return?) When I helped a manufacturing consulting firm shift to value-based fees, the owners told me that a 3:1 return for their clients was considered outstanding.

Value is in the eye of the beholder, which is why it is reached collaboratively with the buyer in conceptual agreement. However, you can suggest and propose additional value as you get to know the buyer and the organization, before creating the proposal. That's what the value distance is about. Remember, too, that behind every business objective is a personal objective, and this is equally important.

As a buyer, my wish to create better teamwork to avoid work duplication and establish a more seamless customer interface is a lofty organizational need. But behind that might well be my personal need to escape spending so much of my time "refereeing" among warring teams and committees. These personal objectives should be discussed because of the increased value they generate.

The total of tangible benefits (which are often annualized), intangible benefits (which have emotional impact), and peripheral benefits (valuable "extras") create a potent value equation. Money is a priority issue and not a resource issue, so the more ROI you present the more likely money will be moved your way. And because we are dealing only with economic buyers, the authority to move that money is present.

When you have a trusting relationship with a true buyer, there is no reason to go anywhere else, to conduct a needs analysis, or to interview bystanders. So let's make sure you know how that's best done.

Notes

1. If you're pricing by time and materials and intend to continue doing that, you don't need this book and I'm frankly surprised you can afford it. A simple letter of agreement can adequately address these relationships.

2. For examples of questions to ask throughout these steps see "101 Questions for Every Sales Situation" in the online appendix for this book.

3. Any current business has these two vital components. See my book, *Million Dollar Referrals* (McGraw-Hill, 2011).

4. Though I'm happy to report that even the legal profession is moving toward value-based fees, and I've had correspondence with the Chief Justice of Western Australia, who is a proponent of this approach. See my book from John Wiley & Sons, *Value-Based Fees*.

2

Five Steps Toward Great Leaps

How to Prepare Yourself and the Client

Determining the Economic Buyer

The economic buyer is the linchpin to any proposal because only he or she can say yes (or no). *You want to avoid those people who can say no but can't say yes*—the gatekeepers. (Later on, we discuss techniques that provide for a choice of yeses, thereby improving your odds hugely.)

I actually had someone (on Twitter, where else?) attempt to argue with me that he is a buyer in his company and has his own budget, yet must get permission from his boss to spend it! No matter what he chooses to call himself or how he prefers to delude himself, he's not a buyer. *True, economic buyers* have the power to spend money on their own authority.

Now, buyers may change roles as the money changes. Someone with a maximum spending grant of $300,000 is not going to be your buyer for a $2 million project. Some consultants actually "outgrow" their buyers as their services become more comprehensive and sophisticated. That's quite fine.

Whenever you receive or generate a lead, don't simply do backflips because someone is interested in your services. Use the interest to quickly determine whether the person involved is a buyer. If they are, we discuss how to develop a trusting relationship in the next segment. But if they're not, then your sole course of action is to explore how that person can lead you to the true buyer.

That may sound mercenary at first blush, but I'll remind you that this is a business, not an avocation. Here are some questions to pursue to test whether someone is a buyer:

1. Whose budget will support this initiative?
2. Who can immediately approve this project?
3. To whom will people look for support, approval, and credibility?
4. Who controls the resources required to make this happen?
5. Who has initiated this request?
6. Who will claim responsibility for the results?
7. Who will be seen as the main sponsor and/or champion?
8. Do you have to seek anyone else's approval?
9. Who will accept or reject proposals?
10. If you and I were to shake hands, could I begin tomorrow?
11. What is the decision-making process for this type of approval?

You don't have to interrogate someone under a bare light-bulb, but you do need to use several of these questions to ascertain

> **Key Point:** The larger the organization, the more the number of economic buyers. They need not be the CEO or owner, but must be able to authorize and produce payment. Committees are never economic buyers.

who is going to approve your eventual proposal. Normally, human resources people and training people are never economic buyers in any major organization. They are usually acting on behalf of a line entity that has requested help in finding resources. The only exceptions are occasionally the executive vice president (or similar title) of HR, but that isn't terribly common, either. (These people are sometimes buyers for commodities, such as training materials, seminars, and so forth.)

As painful or awkward as it may seem (no doubt some of you reading this are refugees from HR), you cannot afford to establish relationships with nonbuyers. You will be seen as their peer, which will completely undermine you with executives, or they will consume your time and never introduce you to anyone who can buy out of fear of being left out. Ironically, many HR people "tasked" with finding consultants (whom they inevitably regard as vendors) are offended that they, themselves, haven't been asked to complete the project seeking external resources. Finally, these folks seldom understand the larger picture, strategy, or sophisticated results.

In other words, it's the La Brea Tar Pits of approval.

You'll also find that committees are next to useless.

First, when someone says, "The committee will have to hear this," you know immediately that that person is not a buyer! Second, few committees have budgets. They are usually recommending agents to the person who *does* have a budget. Third, there is almost always someone on the committee who is the actual decision maker or a key recommender (KR). These key recommenders can be highly useful because, unlike other gate-keepers, they see their role as introducing high-quality resources to important buyers.

So either find the decision maker or KR on the committee, or find the person to whom the committee is reporting its recommendations.

In small companies, the buyer is the owner, founder, or president, with rare exception. That's also true in medium-sized companies, but here you might also find a general manager or a similar position. In large companies, you might find buyers all over the place, and their status seldom is reflected on their business card. For example, in banks *everyone* is a vice president, even if they merely keep the lines orderly, but virtually no one has any real authority (try to get a small business loan). However, in Merck, a Fortune 50 company, I had dozens of buyers in a dozen years, and one who approved $250,000 in projects three years in a row had the modest title of "director of international development."

Although you may assume that in large organizations the heads of business units and large staff areas are always buyers, you can add to that hundreds of people who happen to have significant budget latitude. So you have to do some groundwork, using the questions above and asking others whom you meet.

Keep this in mind: You have value that can significantly improve the client's condition. It's incumbent on you to try to implement that value to achieve that end. The sole manner in which to do so efficaciously is through someone who can completely agree to, approve, and fund a project. If you lose sight of that goal, then no amount of speed or enthusiasm will compensate for your ending up in the wrong port.

Of the five ways in which most consultants fail to sustain themselves, the inability to find the true buyer is one.[1]

Developing Trusting Relationships

A trusting relationship in this context is one in which the economic buyer and the consultant interact as peers, exploring whether a project makes sense and, if so, how to proceed as partners. Such a relationship is required prior to successful proposals because the linchpin of the proposal and the basis for your fees—conceptual agreement—cannot be thoroughly obtained without trust.

If I am to share my objectives, agree on metrics, stipulate value, raise honest objections, cite probably risks, and so on, I must trust you. These are not issues that are plastered on the walls or broadcast on the elevators.

Here are the hallmarks of a trusting relationship:

- Volunteering information, for example, "We've had a hard time recruiting minority candidates for key positions, and it's a thorn in our side."

- Sharing background, for example, "I never would have come here myself, except the COO changed and the new one had worked with me prior and I respect him enormously."

- Allowing and entertaining pushback, for example, "Your idea that we need to take 'heroic measures' outside of our own compensation criteria is risky but perhaps inevitable."

- Agreements are met, for example, meetings are uninterrupted, calls are returned, promised documentation is provided, and so on.

- Advice is sought, for example, "How would you organize such a search effort if you had *carte blanche*?"

- Value is admitted, for example, "We've never looked at it that way before, and you've just provided a significant new route for us."

Sometimes trusting relationships are built in 20 minutes, and sometimes it requires three meetings. (If it takes months, it was not meant to be.) *One of the greatest mistakes consultants make is to hurry through what they believe to be the "preliminaries" in order to get to the "deal" and the proposal.* Any proposal that is not the result of conceptual agreement based on a trusting relationship is inauthentic, and the odds of it being successful are a fraction as high as when done the right way.

Sometimes you can generate "instant trust." This has probably happened to you in the past on occasion, and here are three underlying principles in a business setting:

1. Platinum reference.

   A peer of the buyer recommends you to the buyer. Their relationship is so strong that your prospective buyer is prepared to instantly respect you and trust you. Think of the conditions under which you make purchases and instantly trust others—these are often due to a trusted colleague or friend's recommendations.[2]

2. Commercially published book.

   This is the "gold standard," and many buyers will swoon and gladly form immediate bonds with a commercially published (*not* self-published) author, especially if the work is well known. Many of my clients rapidly entered into the proposal phase with me *even though they hadn't actually read my book!* That was fine with

---

Glossary

Trusting relationships are those wherein either party trusts the other with their "wallet"—ideas, information, insights, innovation.

me, and I certainly didn't test them on the contents of Chapter 8.

3. Well-known intellectual property (IP) and/or visibility.

Sometimes you may be featured in the media as an expert, or you may be responsible for a model or methodology that is highly popular. Someone I mentor is usually called for media interviews on his specialty—crisis management, for example.

These are three methods for instant credibility. They don't always work, and in any case most of us will be faced with trudging up a steeper hill. Here are five tips that will help you create trusting relationships when you don't have access to the express lanes:

1. Offer value from the outset.

Those who tell you to refrain from "giving away" your intellectual property are either paranoid or don't have any IP that others would find valuable in any case. Why else would I write more than 40 books, encouraging people to learn, apply, and benefit from my techniques? Because they want more. Many of you reading this book will purchase others, or attend a speech I'm giving, or join my Mentor Program, listen to a teleconference, and so forth. What you want to create is the belief that, "If I'm getting this much from an initial meeting, how much more would I derive from partnering on a project?"

2. Listen and ask provocative questions.

Never give a "pitch." Throw "elevator pitches" down the shaft. Never enter any buyer's office with a PowerPoint presentation or a "card deck." One buyer, who spoke to me for 45 minutes straight with only a brief "Really?" or "Hmmmm" from me (to prove I wasn't asleep with my eyes open) finally told me that he believed I was "the first consultant who ever sat in his office who really understood his business." (He became a $565,000 client over the course of five years.)

3. Look and act like a success.

Wear an expensive suit. Don't take out a dollar pen to write notes in a battered notebook. Your shoes should be shined, you hair well styled, and your accessories intelligent. If you're driving to the client and don't have a nice car, then rent one. Lest this seem superficial to you, permit me to remind you that successful people want to be around successful people, and they will more readily trust people who are manifestly successful. Wouldn't you? I'm not taking skiing lessons from the instructor with battered equipment who can't afford a lift ticket.

4. Never dumb down your language.

This is among the worst advice in the history of sales and marketing, and it's usually espoused by those who seek to bring others down to their level of inarticulateness. Use metaphor, example, metonymy, analogy, and "war stories." Study enough to be conversant in the buyer's business (e.g., in a bank know what a loan defalcation means), but you don't have to be the content expert (because the client already is).

5. Stay in the moment and don't think about "selling."

Have a conversation. Focus on the fact that you are evaluating whether you want to work with this buyer just as the buyer is evaluating whether to work with you. Don't put undue pressure on yourself or the circumstances. Patience trumps pressure. You want to be seen as a calm resource, not a vendor desperate for a sale.

Now let's look at the next step in our leap.

Establishing Outcome-Based Business Objectives

Most objectives that govern projects really aren't objectives. They tend to be deliverables, *especially* if they are created by the training or human resources functions. They are also often metrics, rather than results.

Here are examples of some truly lousy project objectives that nonetheless often stick their ugly heads above the water:

- Run a three-day leadership conference.
- Provide coaching for one day per week.
- Create a customer call processing of 15 people per hour.
- Counsel Mike on how to better manage his time.
- Develop more staff confidence.
- Take us from "good to great."[3]

Now I'll turn them into true business outcomes that mean something in terms of eventual value, which we cover later in this chapter:

- Leaders will voluntarily share resources and information and cease creating duplication and client confusion.
- Enable Mary to present corporate results to the media without reading a prepared script and to answer spontaneous questions rapidly and to the satisfaction of the questioner.
- Improve the speed of customer processing without diminishing quality.
- Enable Mike to get his job completed to his boss's satisfaction in less than 45 hours per week.

- Push decision making down to frontline levels so that there are fewer approvals, faster response time, and less failure work.
- Maximize our ability to _____ (fill in the blank).

You might disagree with some of my wording, which is fine, but I think you'll agree that we're not talking about results that have an impact on the business and not simply tasks.

About 99.99 percent of all RFPs (requests for proposals) you'll ever receive are really arbitrary alternatives packaged as if they are projects. They specify how much time, duration, how many people, how many sites, and so on. They are invariably created by a cohort of low-level people who evaluate all the wrong things—tasks versus outcomes. (Will you eat lunch on-site? Will you cut your bread horizontally or diagonally?) This is why it's rarely sensible to respond to RFPs, because you're never dealing with a buyer and the source is always looking for how much you'll charge by the hour.

These 11 questions best elicit true business objectives:

1. What is the ideal outcome you'd like to experience?
2. What results are you trying to accomplish?
3. What better product/service/customer/employee condition are you seeking?
4. Why are you seeking to do this (work/project/engagement)?
5. How would the operation be different as a result of this work?
6. Why are you considering this project (to improve what)?
7. How would image/repute/credibility be improved?
8. What harm (e.g., stress, dysfunction, turf wars) would be alleviated?
9. How much would you gain on the competition as a result?

10. How would your value proposition be improved?

11. How would you most easily justify this investment?

A few of these questions honestly answered in a trusting relationship will provide your project objectives (which is why an economic buyer's attention is all you need—no needs analysis, endless interviews, and so on). Ironically, lower level people and gatekeepers usually can't give you the proper answers because they don't know them!

Most projects have a handful of objectives, from two to six. A single objective is usually too narrowly focused on an alternative (e.g., place an interview in publication X), and too many are usually a gallimaufry of vague intentions (e.g., expand in Europe while developing our domestic management team and improving quality).

Each objective can provide a variety of values to the client, so even a few can result in substantial impact, which in turn justifies significant fees.

The best way to rapidly move a buyer from tasks and arbitrary alternatives to genuine business outcomes is to ask, "Why?"

"We want someone to run a weekend strategy retreat in October."

"Why?"

"Our strategy isn't being universally implemented uniformly."

Glossary

Objectives are business outcomes and results that have substantial impact on the products, services, and relationships of the enterprise, and which can be measured. They may be new opportunities reached or problems solved.

"So your need is to accelerate your ability to meet your strategic goals on a global basis?"

"That's the reason."

Note how much more value is inherent in that restated objective, and how much more latitude exists for meeting it than a simple weekend of moving items from one easel sheet to another!

Establishing Metrics for Progress and Success

The basic question to ask ourselves here is, "How would you know it if you tripped over it?"

There is far too much going on in terms of "feeling confident" or "clarifying" or "believing." But you don't know that those are not proper indicators. You wouldn't know them if you tripped over them. (The only way you know that I'm more confident is that I ask you fewer questions, confront buyers with better rebuttals, speak up forcefully at meetings, and so forth.)

The measures of success will underscore the direct role that your contributions have played in reaching the objectives. There can be more than one metric for a given objective:

- Objective: Increase repute in the community.
- Measures:
  - Increased, positive coverage in local media.

Glossary

Metrics are indicators of progress or success, which anyone can use to determine that key goals have been reached. They reside in observed behavior and/or evidence in the environment.

- Local service club bestows accolades and awards.
- Higher levels of local, highly qualified job candidates.

Some of the questions you can ask include:

- How will you know we've accomplished your intent?
- How, specifically, will the operation be different when we're done?
- How will you measure this?
- What indicators will you use to assess our progress?
- Who or what will report on our results (against the objectives)?
- Do you already have measures in place that you intend to apply?
- What is the rate of return (on sales, investment, etc.) that you seek?
- How will we know how the public, employees, and/or customers perceive it?
- Each time we talk, what standard will tell us we're progressing?
- How would you know it if you tripped over it?

Some metrics are anecdotal, not scientific. That's okay, as long as you and the buyer agree on who is doing the measuring and how. For example, a divisional general manager sought greater team collaboration with fewer turf battles. When I asked how he'd know this was accomplished, he told me, "I won't be seeing warring factions every day in my office for whom I have to serve as referee."

That was good enough for me and for him.

Metrics are vital during the project so that there are early indications of anyone falling behind. That way you can alert your buyer, who has the real clout and authority, that some attitudes and behaviors require changing. "You and I agreed that a key metric was that all five service areas embraced the new technology by April 1, but as of March 15, the call center has not had one person attend any meetings and the manager has not returned calls. You need to change his attitude about this."

A professor at the University of Wisconsin posited four levels of measurement in 1959:

1. Reactions of learners.
2. Increased knowledge of learners.
3. Behavioral change of learners.
4. Results of the behavioral changes.

HR people still speak about this as if it's the Holy Grail more than a half-century later, and training magazines quote it as scripture. Unfortunately, it was superficial and academic in 1959, and it still is today. The *only* measure that matters is improved results—an improved client condition, in this case represented by objectives met and validated by key metrics. Those metrics are, in turn, based on empirical evidence in the environment that can be readily identified.

Here's another way to view the evidence you need:

Beliefs—Enlightened self-interest

Attitudes—Normative pressure

Behaviors—Coercion

We tend to "whack" bad behaviors, but that only lasts as long as the whacker has a larger stick and is present. We tend to try to sway attitudes through normative pressure ("be one of the in crowd"), but such entreaties are inconsistent and opinion is fickle.

Only through addressing enlightened self-interest can we prompt belief and attitude changes that will be reflected in behavior changes, which produce new results. Therefore, most projects will include elements on achieving commitment, and not merely compliance (whack), and will be measured by an improved resultant client condition.

Try *not* to choose metrics (or objectives) that specify a level of performance, for example, a 3 percent margin improvement or six new customers per month. Instead, create movement in the right direction: Maximize the margins as measured by the profit per customer improving, and maximize new customers per salesperson as measured by additional signed contracts monthly.

Note that metrics and objectives may sometimes overlap and resemble each other. You may have an objective of "12 new accounts," but I'd rather see "improvement in number of new accounts" as measured by monthly registrations. There are too many variables outside of your control to commit to specific numbers. The key is to arrive at a range in the objectives step that pleases the buyer (conceptual agreement) and to take the conservative end of that range.

Sometimes, "success" is years away, for example, "create a European operation within the next five years." Your contribution may only be for a portion of that time. But your metrics will cover the elements essential during your tenure—hiring five European account managers, translating materials into the six major languages, and so forth.

Establishing Value and Impact

The most difficult part of conceptual agreement for most consultants is establishing value. That's because they believe that the objectives constitute the value—and they probably will, if we left it at that.

But what I've learned is that there is a multiplicity of value emerging from most individual objectives. The more we cajole the buyer into agreeing as to what they are *and the impact on the buyer personally and the organizations professionally*, the higher fees we can justify in terms of return on investment (ROI).

Here's a single, stereotypical objective that most people would also say is the value derived: Increase profit.

However, potential value from reaching the objective of increased profit includes:

- Pay higher dividends to investors.
- Invest in business expansion.
- Increase bonuses to retain top talent.
- Be more competitive in hiring.
- Pay down debt.
- Improve stock price.

You get the idea. By prompting and provoking the buyer, you can derive a great deal of value from each objective. And it's the value that will be used to justify the fees you charge, not the objectives.

Questions to ask to generate value statements include:

- What will these results mean for your organization?
- How would you assess the actual return (ROI, ROA, ROS, ROE, etc.)?[4]
- What would be the extent of the improvement (or correction)?
- How will these results impact the bottom line?
- What are the *annualized* savings (first year might be deceptive)?
- What is the intangible impact (on repute, safety, comfort, etc.)?
- How would you, personally, be better off or better supported?

- What is the scope of the impact (on customers, employees, vendors)?
- How important is this compared to your overall responsibilities?
- What if this fails?

The proposal's ultimate fees will be based on these relationships, *if understood by the buyer in this preparation stage:*

$$\frac{\text{Tangible Benefits} \times \text{Annualization} + \text{Intangible Benefits} \times \text{Emotional Impact} + \text{Peripheral Benefits}}{\text{Fee}} = \text{Value}$$

The tangible benefits (increased profit, decreased downtime) times the years the benefits will accrue and grow; plus the intangible benefits (be seen as a leader, discard unpleasant work) times their emotional impact; plus the peripheral benefits (easier to attract talent, better media treatment); over your fee, equals the value or ROI for the client.

A relatively few objectives can yield dozens of value statements, especially when you consider professional, personal, and peripheral, the three Ps of value. The higher these are *in the buyer's eyes and with the buyer's concurrence*, the higher your fee can be while still generating significant value.

Glossary

Value is the degree of positive impact personally, professionally, and peripherally that objectives that are met generate. It is the soul of the project, the reason that major investments can be readily justified.

Commodities, such as training programs or coaching days, don't afford as much value because they are about time and materials and are easily compared to others' prices. But true projects are never commodities and never comparable (which is why you should generally avoid RFPs, as discussed earlier).

Buyers, especially highly assertive and fast-moving senior people, tend to think in terms of tasks being accomplished and goals being reached. You have to "slow them down" a bit so that you can remind them and gain agreement on the results of those tasks that help to reach those goals. The intangible benefits are especially important, because circumstances such as increased safety, reduced stress, greater comfort, and increased aesthetics can be highly powerful drivers and highly regarded value. (This is why architects undercharge—they focus on the building extension rather than the improved quality of life for the family.)

Value, like beauty, may be in the eye of the beholder, but it's nonetheless discussable and mutually appreciated. This final step in conceptual agreement is an integral part in preparing the client for an acceptable proposal and is absolutely vital, yet often rushed through or completely ignored.

Here is a summary of the key elements before we move on to ensuing that these approaches reach the right eyes and ears:

- Never provide a proposal for a gatekeeper or intermediary, even if that person promises to "sell" it for you. That person won't have your passion and will fold under pressure. He or she has more to lose than you do.

- Forge a trusting relationship first, so that the buyer is comfortable sharing facts, opinions, needs, and desires. Invest as much time as needed to develop that bond.

- Clearly understand and differentiate among objectives, metrics, and value. Focus on the multiple value and impact that any one objective may represent.
- Reaffirm each item in these three areas with the buyer. Ensure that you have true conceptual agreement prior to creating any proposal.
- Never discuss fees at this point. The key is what the buyer's improved conditions will be. The fees and subsequent ROI will come later. *If you are talking about fees or price at this point, you've lost control of the discussion.*

Notes

1. Along with failing to build a trusting relationship; failing to provide options; failing to establish definitive next steps; and failing to charge high enough fees. All can be remedied with this book!

2. For details on this highest quality of all trusting mechanisms and referrals, see my book *Million Dollar Referrals* (McGraw-Hill, 2011).

3. With apologies to Jim Collins and his fine book, too many companies blindly want to embrace the mantra and not the meaning.

4. Returns on investment, assets, sales, equity.

Avoiding Gatekeepers, Intermediaries, and Goblins

Accepting Rejection and Rejecting Acceptance

Utilizing Mutual, Enlightened Self-Interest

The best way to traverse gatekeeperland is to treat gatekeepers with respect but at arm's-length distance. The last thing in the world you need is to be seen as a peer of the intermediary. That will doom you no less than the Death Star from Star Wars in terms of habitable life in that prospect.

Consequently, you must learn to accept rejection and reject acceptance. We all know about the former. This is the marketing business and many people say no. (The best hitters in baseball, even on steroids, only hit about three out of every 10 times at bat.

That's a 70 percent failure rate.) So we inure ourselves to this or we drink heavily.

However, we don't fully appreciate rejecting acceptance. Low-level people can feel important by interacting with outsiders directly, and so in that context you are raw meat for the relationship predators. Keep your distance. Work with gatekeepers to the extent that they can help you with the express lane to the buyer.

I call this "mutual, enlightened self-interest" because everyone wins.

If the gatekeeper chooses to accompany you to the buyer—introducing you and vouching for you—that's wonderful, because he or she will get credit for your brilliance and you will probably wind up collaborating on parts of the project implementation.

But if the gatekeeper prefers to send you along by yourself, staying out of the line of fire, that is also fine. Your retirement plan, merit increases, coveted parking space, and daily affiliation needs are not vested in that prospect. You can afford to take the flak where the gatekeeper may be gun-shy, and understandably so.

What you can't allow, however, is the gatekeeper to block you by not raising the gate. So trying to create a mutually beneficial advantage is the first avenue to explore.

When I first began working with Merck as a client, Art Strohmer was a human resources manager. He saw his job as connecting appropriate and top-quality external resources with internal areas of relevant need. Any services he purchased from me were minor, but he consistently set up six-figure projects for me with line people who had the need and the budget—the true economic buyers. (Art is retired today for many years, but we still exchange holiday cards and the occasional e-mail.)

Here are best and worst practices in terms of trying to build mutual self-interest so that a gatekeeper leads you to a buyer:

TABLE 3.1 Mutual Self-Interest Best and Worst Pracitces

Best Practices	Worst Practices
Focus on the process of the buying decision	Focus on content of the project
Brief meetings with clear agendas	Brainstorming and meals
Clarify your need to meet person with budget	Be vague about your next steps
Never offer a proposal or agreement	Provide proposal for review
Never allow to market for you internally	Assign as intermediary with buyer
Never rely on their views or interpretations	Assume they are accurate
Do not wait, create your own time frames	Rely on their "right time"

Size up your gatekeepers quickly. If they are confident and assertive, they should be ready, willing, and able to lead you to the land of the buyers. But if you find that's not the case, then move on to the techniques in the following parts of this chapter.

Remember that enlightened self-interest doesn't involve anything unethical or illegal. You don't bribe gatekeepers to be introduced to the buyer. But you can find common ground where the gatekeeper sees your introduction to the buyer as a huge personal gain:

- You represent a key resource that the gatekeeper found.
- The gatekeeper gets the credit for taking the initiative.
- A favorite priority of the buyer will be addressed.

Case Study: International Paper

Many years ago, two of us were assigned the client-service role by our consulting firm for a major client, International Paper, in Georgia. This was the kind of plant at the time that you could smell for miles downwind, and where the vegetation for three miles had a chemical coating, and cars in the parking lot were rusting in front of your eyes.

My partner, Ronnie, and I were never able to expand the sale past the gatekeeper we had inherited, a training guy named Don. But Don was superb at getting us to buy him free meals during our visits.

One day, just to break the tedium, Ronnie and I bet on how many free meals Don would mooch from us over two days on-site. The bet was $50, and Ron had nine meals while I had eight.

As Don drove us back to the airport at the end of the second day, we had had eight meals, so at least I had won $50. But suddenly Don said, "You two have at least 90 minutes to spare, and there's a McDonald's with a drive-through over there, why don't we give it a try?"

Out of nowhere I said, "A drive-through isn't a meal!"

Ronnie replied, "I guess if you chew it and digest it, it must be a meal."

And that's how we never got to the economic buyer *and* I lost $50.

- Someone will have to be the champion of the internal resources.
- There may be company-wide publicity and acclaim.
- A promotion could hinge on the project's success.

- The gatekeeper can learn your methodology.
- The gatekeeper has done this before, so there is precedent.

If the intermediary decides to be part of the meeting with the buyer, acknowledge his or her help to this point but run the meeting using your agenda and intent. Remember that some buyers might not want to disclose everything in front of a subordinate, and your goal is to establish a trusting relationship with the buyer, so ultimately you'll want to meet one-on-one. Keep the gatekeeper apprised of the general direction and issues, so that he or she feels included.

If the intermediary decides not to participate in the initial meeting with the buyer, then make sure that he or she provides a solid introduction in person, by phone, or by e-mail (in that order or preference), and again pay that person the respect of being apprised of the progress.

Using Guile and Other Art Forms

Sometimes the other party just isn't that enlightened despite your best efforts. In this case, you need to invoke some guile, or artistry, to ease your way on down the road.

If the first technique works about 50 percent of the time, this one works about 25 percent of the time. You need to make an unrebuttable excuse to meet the true buyer.

My favorite is this: "Ethically, as you can imagine, in order to provide a proposal for any project I must speak to the person whose fiduciary responsibility includes evaluating the return on their budgetary investment. I must hear from his or her lips what expectations they have to ensure they are not being unreasonable or underestimating the return. Once that's established, I'm happy to work with you on the implementation of whatever project emerges."

Picture a "comma" after "ethically" when you say this. The statement truly gives people cause for pause. Here are some likely follow-up statements.

"But no other consultant has asked us to do this."

"Frankly, I'm shocked that you'd consider any consultant who doesn't want to fulfill this ethical obligation, and that's why you need me."

Or:

"Sandy Jones is very busy and has tasked[1] me to evaluate resources."

"I'm very busy, too, and my intent is to evaluate whether Ms. Jones and I can work as partners on this project."

Or:

"I can tell you everything you need to know and then take your proposal to Sandy Jones."

"My experience over the years is that the buyer always has objectives that others aren't privy to and/or that we end up developing together. If this project is undertaken, and Ms. Jones feels she's been misinformed or the direction isn't consistent, she's going to react poorly to you, not to me. It's not my retirement plan that's vested here."

You may feel that these are strong statements and they are, but you have *nothing to lose* when the gatekeeper keeps sitting on the gate. You should always point out: "We have three options before us. The two of us can go to Ms. Jones as a team, which is fine with me. However, if there is the chance of any backlash, I'm happy to go alone and take the hit, after your introduction. The third option is your going alone, and that's not on the table because it's unfair of me to expect you to do my marketing for me." (Which of course they won't do very well or passionately in any case.)

This is useful to remember when you're faced a few times a year with the rubric: "The committee makes the decision, and I have to present to them." Very, very few committees decide. The members usually recommend to the person who formed it, who may be a part of it or may not be. So you're still better off trying to find the true buyer. But the same guile can be applied: "The committee will ask you questions that you won't be able to answer, so why don't we simply arrange for me to appear in front of the committee with you?"

This may all seem as if they are merely alternate appeals to self-interest, but they are "after the fact." That is, they are used when the gatekeeper refuses original appeals to self-interest, which are positive (look good, take credit). These art forms are really based on fear (you'll be asked questions you can't answer, what if the buyer is unhappy with the project) and propriety (there is an ethical necessity).

The points you make with this language are perfectly valid. I'm not talking about "guile" in the sense of trickery or persiflage. I'm simply suggesting that you can find a side door to the fortress when the drawbridge is up and the moat seems active with large reptiles.

Bear in mind that for years consultants have educated gatekeepers incorrectly and have bestowed on them pseudo-power—the power of means over ends, which is commonly known as *bureaucracy*. You have to overcome that by introducing new learning and new facts.

The point is that *only a true, economic buyer can provide the relationship, conceptual agreement, and approval to create the partnership you need.*

Any proposal that does not go to an economic buyer is pointless. Even if accepted, it will be changed, altered, and often ignored by underlings, minions, and functionaries. If you've arrived at this point, where a representative from a legitimate prospect is communicating with you, then don't give up the ship by allowing low-level people on board who promise to pilot the craft into the harbor.

You'll wind up on the rocks.

Here are the key points to bring to bear when a gatekeeper is not amenable to self-interest to introduce you to the buyer:

- Ethics: It's a professional responsibility, and one of mutual respect.

- Precedent: What's probably been the case in the past is no longer appropriate.

- Fear: What if something goes wrong after you take responsibility for vetting and accepting the proposal?

- Ignorance: All buyers have both personal and professional objectives they likely have not shared with subordinates.

- Partnership: You are evaluating the organization as a client, so there is a reciprocity here. (Most consultants walk in as supplicants rather than potential partners.)

- Speed: If you want to get this done then I must talk to the person who can approve it instantly.

- Clout: Inevitably, the buyer will have to champion this at the outset and perhaps through the implementation. That has to begin now.

- Credibility: This project cannot be seen as a human resources or training program or it will not receive proper support from line management. (If they don't believe that, firmly pull their heads out of the sand.)

Using Explosives

Sometimes both enlightenment and guile fail. A human resources manager told me that I'd work through her or not at all. For me, that's an easy choice. There are people who are threatened, turf-defenders, insecure, envious, confused, and just malicious.

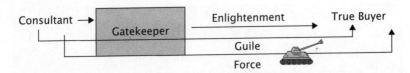

FIGURE 3.1   Circumventing gatekeepers

Unfortunately, you find them more often among gatekeepers than true buyers. But that makes sense, because real buyers have real power.

So when there is no side door to the fortress and the gators are swimming by, you may want to try to blow a hole in the works. You'll be successful only about 10 percent of the time, but that's still better than the zero you'll wind up with by submitting proposals to low-level people. See Figure 3.1.

This is a last resort, but because you're not going to get this business anyway, you really have no downside. The worst thing you can do is waste time developing a relationship and submitting a proposal to someone who can say no but can't say yes.

Now, what do I mean by "blowing up" the gatekeeper? I mean that you should feel free to pursue the buyer directly, because you may well know who he or she is by now or you can readily find out. You should cease to worry about the gatekeeper's feelings or directions.

Many people become alarmed at this point that the gatekeeper will undermine the ensuing project if you are successful finding and partnering with the economic buyer. Let me assure you that no subordinate is going to overtly undermine a superior's project, and your relationship with the buyer will be strong enough so that you can easily point to any such interference and have it corrected.

The language you can use with the gatekeeper can be something like these statements (*not* questions):

- Since I've explained my need to meet with the buyer and you've been unwilling or unable to create an introduction,

---

A Digression

I realize that my stance here is somewhat harsh. After all, most of you can point to people in human resources, training, or learning and development who have helped you and perhaps even managed to buy from you with their own budget. But to quote Damon Runyon, "The race is not always to the swift nor the battle to the strong, but that's the way to bet."

If you find a hundred dollars when you're walking to work, you can count yourself lucky, but I doubt you'd quit your job to support your family by searching for money in the street. There are always exceptions, but they prove the rule. I'm interested in your well-being and in your capacity to feed your family. I don't care if the human resources profession takes exception or dislikes me.

You cannot succeed in this business by catering to and dealing with low-level people unless it's to work with them to quickly introduce you to legitimate economic buyers. If you don't believe that, then you're wasting your time and money in this profession.

I'm going to attempt that on my own. I'll mention our earlier discussions and the fact that you've been truly helpful.

- I have some other avenues I can pursue with the buyer (you can use a name here, of course), and I'm going to try some of them. Do you want me to mention our discussions or not?

- I'm sorry, but my policy and experience in creating successful outcomes demands that I see the buyer, and we have an impasse here. I respect your position, but I'm going to have to take other steps.

At this point, you find the buyer by:

- Asking others you may have met for an introduction.
- Sending a note (see below).
- Arranging to meet at an event where you know that he or she will be present.

I prefer a hard-copy personal note to e-mail, because it stands out more in a crowd these days. Here is an example of such a note. You do not want to criticize the gatekeeper, nor do you want to make a "pitch." Remember, you simply want to gain a meeting with the decision maker. That is your next, small, "yes."

Dear Mr. Watson,

I've been meeting with Randy Chase, who has asked for a proposal regarding my services to help with your expansion plans into new markets. Randy has explained what's needed, and, at this point, I believe I can fulfill those needs.

However, it's become apparent that you are the person with fiduciary responsibility, and it's unethical for me to provide a proposal without hearing from you directly about your objectives, expectations, and desired outcomes. We can accomplish that in a brief visit, and I'll be in your area several times over the next month.

I'll call on Friday at 10 A.M. to set something up that's mutually convenient and will enable me to generate an accurate proposal with detailed ROI based on your inputs and information. If that date and time are not good for you, please suggest another or contact me at the number on this letterhead.

Looking forward to meeting you.

Sincerely,

When you call, and you get a secretary or voice mail, say, "This is Joyce Randall and I'm calling as promised," and nothing more. My suggestion is to call three times, and then write a final note expressing your disappointment that you were unable to meet.

Never burn your bridges, but don't spend excess time trying to make this happen. It works about 10 percent of the time, so it's worth some limited effort. Don't copy the gatekeeper, by the way. You're flying at a higher altitude now.

Avoiding Delegation

In many cases, consultants reach the economic buyer but quickly find themselves out in the cold draft of the hallway again. They reach the summit, but then fall off.

The reason is that, instead of attempting to develop a relationship with the buyer, the consultant is too scared, too subordinated, too insecure, and doesn't establish a peer connection. So the buyer says something like, "I'm not sure we can use your help or not, but why not talk to my HR director who knows more about this than I do, and see what she says?" And the consultant trots down to HR, hearing the "clunk" of the gates of the cathedral closing forever behind.

The buyer says these things for the following reasons:

- You are talking about deliverables, not results, and the buyer isn't going to make decisions about commodities.
- You talk in jargon, which the buyer identifies as the unique vernacular of HR.
- The buyer legitimately believes that the HR people can provide advice and you do nothing to dissuade or counter that erroneous belief.

- The buyer is unimpressed with your language, approach, or look, and this is the easiest way to get you out of the office quickly.

All of this can be avoided, but you'll have to "consultant up." (I'm attempting gender neutrality here.) Here are your steps.

1. Focus on building the relationship. Don't launch into a "pitch." Never bring visual aids. Adjust to the buyer's style.

2. Don't feel as if this is a final exam. If the buyer says, "Well, what can you do for us?," say, "I don't know, why don't we discuss your current challenges and priorities?"

3. Discuss "what" but not "how." The former will stimulate interaction about key concerns but stop short of offering solutions, free consulting, or opportunity for the buyer to say, "That won't work here."

4. Provide value immediately. For example, tell the buyer, "In my experience there are three keys to retention of top talent. Are you using all three to your maximum ability here?" Or provide a diagnostic and ask which of three circles or four quadrants (or whatever) the buyer's organization occupies, and whether it needs to maintain that position or change.

5. Stress that these are strategic issues not suited for subordinates, whose orientation is tactical.

6. Point out that whenever you suggest major change, people will resist it, unsure of their role, so their feedback is often more self-serving than organizationally oriented.

7. Indicate that HR people are often resentful because they are upset that they didn't think of your intervention first, or hadn't done it successfully themselves, or weren't chosen this time.

In the worst case, here is the language to use:

I'm happy to interview whomever you like. I've found that what I hear is often different or antithetical to what you and I discuss, so let's agree on a date for us to get back together once I see your people. How is next Thursday at 10?

This combination of preventive and contingent action should keep you safe from delegation.

However, there are times when "legitimate" delegation will be requested. The buyer may sincerely want you to talk to some senior people or frontline people whom he or she believes can help in framing the proposal. In that case, agree to the steps (provided they are not laborious, lengthy, or quasi-consulting work) but absolutely insist on the debrief period so that you can finalize a true conceptualized agreement with the buyer.

But the overarching issue here is that consultants *allow themselves* to be delegated. Focus on these causes not from the buyer's perspective, but from your own ability to reconcile them.

Low self-esteem: You feel that you don't deserve to be there, that you're not the equal of the buyer, that you're an impostor. Therefore, you take whatever measures are necessary not to "divulge" who you really are, which means you accept virtually any buyer suggestion or direction.

Fear of losing business: Even experienced, successful consultants seem to think that they desperately need every piece of business and can't afford to lose any "sale," no matter how many concessions and compromises they have to make. This is seldom true, but these subordinate behaviors are what put you in that fearful position of not having enough business.

A love affair with methodology: You are so passionate about the techniques and approaches you've developed that your default position is to dive into it and discuss it from the inside out. Nothing, with the possible exception of vacation photos, bores others more. Focus on the other party's results, not your inputs.

Poor business acumen: If you can't talk about ROI, margins, EBITDA, and valuation, then you can't speak "executive." You must acquaint yourself and become conversant in the language of the executive suite. (Stop using terms such as *C-Level,* which is a term used by lower level people, for example.)

Failure to be "in the moment": Buyers can go in many directions, and you can't stick with a script or choreography. You have to listen, understand why the buyer is going in a certain direction, and work to return to the port of call you have in mind. That may take a while. Listen for comments, which you can leverage to make your points and cement the relationship.

Failure to set an agenda: Here's a great opening line: "I know your time, like my time, is precious. I'd like to cover three things today and I'm sure you have some key issues, as well. Why don't we agree on those and use our time accordingly?" This immediately makes you a peer, setting the agenda, and enables you to direct the conversation to your best interests. Many promising meetings simply run out of time because the consultant doesn't properly manage the time. You can always come back, but the longer things take, the more bad things can happen. Thus, it's best to try to obtain a decent time frame (60–90 minutes) that is uninterrupted so that you can attempt to establish the proper relationship and trust, and gain conceptual agreement during that period.

Ensuring Support

Before we enter the architecture of the proposal, let's focus for a bit on ensuring that we garner and maintain the support we need. To this point, we've avoided or circumvented gatekeepers and achieved conceptual agreement with the economic buyer, based on the trusting relationship we've created.

Prior to creating the proposal, discuss with the buyer these five issues:

1. What are the accountabilities and roles the buyer accepts?

   There must be a key person within the client who can shake loose bottlenecks and champion the right behavior. That should be the buyer (and can also be additional people). Does the buyer understand and commit to those duties, particularly at the outset of the project? The buyer has to walk the talk (demonstrate desired behaviors) *as well as* talk the walk (communicate progress and accomplishment).

2. Are there any barriers that haven't been discussed yet?

   Sometimes the normal course of discussion does not include potentially formidable barriers, such as entrenched department heads, competing projects, technology change, and so forth. What can the buyer foresee that the two of you should be planning to prevent or mitigate at the outset?

3. Who are the key influencers?

   There are people who can informally lend weight and momentum to projects and who should be co-opted early. These may be sales leaders, union officials, popular managers, and so forth. Identify who they are with the buyer, and make plans to involve them in steering

---

Case Study in Resistance

When Hewlett-Packard was still making most of its profit from, of all things, printer ink, the head of the printer operation was a law unto himself. No matter what his peers agreed to, he would often choose to go his own way, confident that he wouldn't be discomfited because he was providing most of the company's bottom line.

Similar dynamics exist in many organizations, albeit to smaller extents. You can just acknowledge them, you have to figure out how the buyer intends to deal with them.

---

committees, important meetings, and so on. Show them how their self-interest will be served and how they'll get credit for progress.

4. Where are the likely early victories?

   Where are the likely best places to consider success? These might be tied in to the key influencers, but they might involve high-performing groups, the top-selling products and services, or particularly attractive markets and geographies. Start with small victories whenever possible to build the momentum.

5. What's on the radar?

   You'll see a line in Proposal I in the next chapter that talks about you and the buyer informing each other of any events or issues that arise that may materially affect success. Now is the time to make the initial request. I've worked on projects where the buyer knew a divestiture was coming but didn't tell anyone, including me!

These final questions and checkpoints are an important transition to the proposal itself. The responses and discussion enable

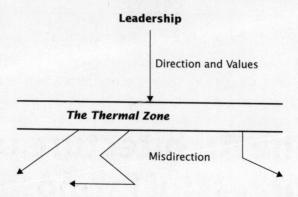

FIGURE 3.2   The thermal zone

you to determine what the buyer's and your accountabilities should be, what time frames make the most sense, what options may be most appealing, and so forth.

In every organization there is a layer—I call it the "thermal zone" (Figure 3.2)—which refracts and redirects things, just as happens in water. That layer comprises key middle managers who *really* run the day-to-day operation, and whose commitment, not mere compliance, is needed for the success of any project.

Therefore, it's best to recognize both them and the circumstances in which they work so that your project isn't refracted out of existence.

Note

1. One of HR's and training's favorite nonverbs.

The Architecture of Successful Proposals

The Million Dollar Consulting® Proposal Structure

The Nine Key Components

There are nine key components in the proposal "architecture" that I've introduced and supported globally over the past 25 years. In this chapter are the latest iterations and examples.

1. Situation Appraisal

> *What:* The situation appraisal is a one- or two-paragraph description of why you and the buyer are discussing the project.
>
> *Why:* The intent is to begin on familiar ground with the premise of the project clear and for the buyer to being nodding "Yes, that's correct."

How: State what the improvement desired is and why it's important to the buyer and/or the organization.

Example

Here's a poor situation appraisal, yet it exemplifies so many of the openings to poor proposals:

> The Acme Company is a provider of financial services located in Cheyenne, which has been in business for 30 years and has a capitalized market value of $800 million.

The Acme buyer knows this! It's nothing novel or new or related to the project. It's irrelevant.
Here's an excellent situation statement:

> The Acme Company has traditionally attracted the best and brightest talent because of its excellent brand and relationships with top schools. However, recent bad publicity over poor financial decisions, the removal of the CEO, and loss of key contacts in top schools have made it imperative to launch an aggressive plan to acquire the best talent in the industry, both at entry and senior levels.

That situation appraisal explains exactly why you've been talking, why the project is urgent, and what the general goals are.

Take a project you're considering, have under way, or have completed, and try writing your own situation appraisal below:

_____

_____

_____

_____

2. Objectives

The next three elements—objectives, metrics, and value—are taken directly from the conceptual agreement elements achieved with the buyer. I prefer to state them as bullet points and not narrative, because they are clearer and more concise.

> *What:* An objective is a business outcome or result that is to be achieved.
>
> *Why:* These are the "improved client conditions" that generate value and, ultimately, ROI.
>
> *How:* State the objectives gained during the conceptual agreement phase, trying not to use specific numbers (e.g., "five new hires," but rather direction, e.g. "maximum new hires").

Example

(continuing with our current example)
The objectives for this project include:

- Reconstruct positive relationships so that we are endorsed by top schools.
- Attract seasoned veterans who see our firm as a "step-up" in prestige.
- Avoid disrupting or threatening current staff.
- Reassure clients and prospects that top talent is present at Acme.
- You will be the leading edge and leader in financial recruitment.

Take a project you're considering, have under way, or have completed, and try writing your own objectives below:

_____

_____

_____

_____

_____

_____

3. Metrics

What: These are the measures of success indicating progress and/or completion.

Why: You and the buyer will use these to guide decisions during the project and to validate your involvement in making the difference.

How: These are taken from conceptual agreement and stated with bullet points, making sure that there is manifest evidence (indicators) for the objectives.

Example

The measures of success for the project will include:

- A minimum of six schools on the top 24 list invite you to recruit on campus.

- Unsolicited resumes are received from top people at competitors.

(continued)

- Unsolicited contacts are made by search firms to provide top talent.
- Your involuntary attrition rate falls below industry averages.
- Clients renew at pre-incident rates and new clients are acquired above industry averages.
- The media create positive stories about your talent success.

Take a project you're considering, have under way, or have completed, and try writing your own metrics below:

_____

_____

_____

_____

_____

_____

4. Value

What: This is the impact on the organization and the buyer for meeting the objectives, as measured by the metrics.

Why: These statements justify the fee by enumerating the ROI and impact.

How: Again in bullet point form, noting that there can be several value statements for any single objective.

Example

The value and impact of achieving the above objectives include:

- Less cost of attracting talent, estimated by you at about 15–25 percent.
- Less current turnover, estimated now at about $400,000 per year.
- Less client turnover, estimated now at $3 million in lost commissions annually.
- New business that should add a minimum of $3 million in commissions.
- Word-of-mouth goodwill for both the company's products and its jobs.
- You being seen as a leading-edge figure in financial recruiting.
- Enhanced media and community relationships.

Note that value is both organizational and professional, and both tangible and intangible, as well as peripheral. Again, the formula we are using is:

$$\frac{\begin{array}{c}\text{Tangible Outcomes} \times \text{Expected Duration} \\ \text{of Outcomes} + \text{Intangible Outcomes} \\ \times \text{Emotional Impact of Intangibles} + \\ \text{Peripheral Benefits} + \\ \text{Variables Positively Effected}\end{array}}{\text{Fixed Investment Required}} = \begin{array}{c}\text{Client's "Good} \\ \text{Deal"}\end{array}$$

Take a project you're considering, have under way, or have completed, and try writing your own value statements below:

_____

_____

_____

_____

_____

_____

5. Methodology and Options

Always try to provide options for clients. This changes the psychology from "Should I do this?" to "*How* should I do this?", which increases your chances for success at least fourfold. Don't go too deeply into methodology (e.g., "focus groups," not "six focus groups in four locations").

> *What:* These are the alternatives that the buyer may select from to reach the objectives, the various roads to the destination. However, some routes provide more value than others, even though the least of them will fulfill the objectives.[1]

> *Why:* To escalate the buyer's decision to add more value and consequently higher fees because of higher ROI. You are adding to the value "above the line" in Figure 3.1, allowing you to increase the fee "below the line," which still increases resultant value.

> *How:* Meet the objectives with the first option, then provide even more value and differentiation in ensuing options.[2]

Example

Option 1, Strategic: We will interview top administrators at your top 24 schools and develop a plan for creating new and strong ties. We will run focus groups comprising current clients to establish the best of your existing services and determine which new ones would be most desirable. We will launch a media campaign of delighted clients, new services, and feature existing top talent. We will create an advisory board of top search firm leadership.

Option 2, Tactical: In addition to Option 1, we will create a monthly, electronic client and prospect newsletter. We will create speaking engagements for the new CEO in front of campus and search audiences. We will monitor current employees for any signs of disaffection of top talent, including observations and personal interviews.

Option 3, Execution: In addition to Options 1 and 2, we will work with your senior management team to develop them in perpetuating this work themselves after our departure. We will create an annual conference of "best practices in talent management in the financial services industry" hosted by your firm. We will revisit once a quarter for the ensuing year to fine-tune and to help you to manage the results.

Note that you can call these options anything you like, including simply "Options 1, 2, and 3." You can also mix and match my particular interventions to suit, as your client and your own taste will differ from my example. But, in theory at least, the differences applicable to any alternative should make sense in the context of that alternative, understanding that prior alternatives are already *inclusive*. Options are not "add-ons," nor are they based on more volume (e.g., interview at 40 schools instead of 24). They are *qualitatively* better, not merely quantitatively larger.

You want to avoid a "take it or leave it" single alternative whenever possible, which should be always.

Take a project you're considering, have under way, or have completed, and try writing your own methodology and options below:

_____

_____

_____

_____

_____

_____

6. Timing

What: This is an estimate and preferably a range of the duration of each of the options barring unforeseen circumstances.

Why: The client deserves to know the extent of your presences and possible disruptions, and you deserve to have a disengagement date set to avoid any possibility of "scope creep" (the buyer requesting that you stick around beyond the objectives being accomplished at no extra fee).

How: State in duration of days, not calendar dates, the estimated time required.

Example

For Option 1, we estimate a 45- to 60-day time frame.

For Option 2, we estimate 60 to 90 days.

For Option 3, we estimate 90 to 120 days, with four quarterly visits in the following 12 months.

These time frames assume that you and we experience no unforeseen delays or postponements. I'm prepared to begin within one week of your acceptance of this proposal.

---

7. Joint Accountabilities

This is one of the most overlooked elements in a proposal. If you concur that you're entering into a partnership with your buyer, then it's only logical that you should each have (and share) accountabilities for success. The project is not something you "do" to the buyer. It's a joint undertaking.

What: These are the responsibilities that you are each in the best position to support individually or that you can best do jointly, and constitute the key areas underlying the success of the project.

Why: By specifying these in the proposal, the buyer is also signing off on his or her personal responsibility and committing to acting in a certain manner, while also being clear on your commitment to critical areas.

How: List those that are unique to the buyer, those that are unique to you, and those that you'll share.

Example

Your accountabilities will include:

- Providing me with access to all key people internally, in colleges, and among your media access.
- Sharing financial details of costs of turnover, loss of customers, acquisition costs, and so forth.
- Free access for me to roam the offices, including security passes, access cards, a private office, and intranet access.
- Providing your personal contact numbers and addresses, weekly debriefs by phone or in person, and responding to my inquiries and requests within 24 hours.
- Honoring the intellectual property and trademarked material I provide for your use.

My accountabilities will include:

- Signing nondisclosure and confidentiality documents.[3]
- Responding to your questions and requests within 90 minutes during Eastern U.S. business hours (put your own service standard in this space).
- Conducting all interviews, focus groups, observations, external interactions personally and with respect for minimizing disruption and concern.
- Meeting all deadlines agreed on and immediately reporting any threats to our progress.

We both will be accountable for:

- Immediately informing the other of any new developments that might materially affect the success of this project.[4]

Take a project you're considering, have under way, or have completed, and try writing equivalent accountabilities for you and the buyer below:

_____

_____

_____

_____

_____

_____

8. Terms and Conditions

This is my favorite part of the proposal! This is the first time—the first time—that the buyer will see the fees. That may be contrary to everything you've ever heard, learned, or practiced, but hear me out. You want the buyer to be nodding assertively and positively throughout this proposal that these are the issues discussed (in conceptual agreement), the options that are valuable and make sense, and that it's time to get started. You want that positive sentiment and momentum to carry right into the fees section.

> _What:_ These are the fees, reimbursements, and terms of payment for the project described herein.
>
> _Why:_ The buyer has now understood the value of the options and can make a reasoned judgment about ROI (return on investment—see Figure 3.1). With value-based fees, there is never a time-based element or meter running, simply a project fee with substantial return.

How: Simply state the fees, reimbursements, and terms, without too much narrative and without confusion. Take into account in your fees the elements in Figure 3.1 from conceptual agreement and the value stated herein.

Example

The fee for Option 1, Strategic, is $176,000.

The fee for Option 2, Tactical, is $211,000.

The fee for Option 3, Execution, is $267,000.

Terms: 50 percent on acceptance of this proposal, and 50 percent 60 days after commencement of work. Alternatively, you may avail yourself of a 10 percent discount with payment in full on acceptance. (NOTE! Some organizations have internal policies stipulating that all discounts must be accepted.)

Expense Reimbursements: We charge expenses as actually accrued and bill at the conclusion of each month. Payment is due upon presentation of our invoice. We charge for reasonable travel, living, and related expenses. We do not charge for administrative support, courier, postage, phone, and so forth.

This project is noncancelable for any reason. You may postpone and reschedule with our approval without penalty so long as you maintain the existing payment schedule. The quality of our work is guaranteed, and if our work is not consistent with the quality expressed in the accountabilities section, we will refund your full fee.

Important Notes:

- The terms are aggressive and I suggest that you always request 50 percent as a deposit, with the balance due in short order, *not* over the course of the project.

- This is as good a time as any to point out that you never want this proposal to go to the legal department, hence, avoid legalese and "boilerplate" such as "third parties shall hold harmless...."

- Specify what your expense policy is and never "nickel and dime" (like lawyers do when they charge you for photocopies).

- Never cite "10 days net" or "30 days net," but rather, "due on presentation" or "on receipt." In worst case, they'll take 30 days but not 60.

- Try to provide a minimum 10:1 return on the client's fee in terms of the value expressed. At these levels, it doesn't matter if Option 1 is $164,000 or $181,000. It doesn't matter. However, ensure that there is sufficient "distance" among options.

Take a project you're considering, have under way, or have completed, and try writing your terms and conditions below:

_____

_____

_____

_____

_____

_____

> ## Case Study: The Insurance Merger
>
> I was hired for the cultural aspects of a huge insurance merger in New York City. The fee was $250,000. I received $125,000 promptly and began work, though my buyer, the executive vice president, never returned a signed copy of the proposal. Sixty days later, I received my second $125,000 on schedule. I completed the project well ahead of deadline in four months, and still had no signed contract.
>
> When I asked the delighted buyer, he told me, "I have authority to sign checks up to $150,000, but I can't sign legal contracts over $100,000 without legal's review. So I took the path of least resistance, figuring you'd be happier with the money and no signed contract than the other way around."
>
> That explains a sentence you'll see in the final segment of the proposal architecture, further on!

9. Acceptance

To steer clear of the legal minefields my proposals are also acceptance vehicles. Thus, after the buyer has read through, agreed to most of what he or she has previously agreed to, and seen attractive options, an immediate decision can be made.

What: The formal and contractual decision is indicated to go forward with the desired option.

Why: Proposals are summations, not explorations. It's important to allow the buyer the opportunity to make an immediate commitment.

How: Include the brief wording and signatory provisions at the conclusion.

Example

Your signature below indicates the acceptance of the option checked and your agreement with all provisions and terms specified in this proposal.

Alternatively, your deposit or full payment and indication of an option will also constitute that acceptance allowing us to begin the project together.

We accept (please check)

__ Option 1   __ Option 2   __ Option 3

and agree to the terms and conditions as specified. We are providing a __ 50 percent deposit or __ full payment less a 10 percent professional discount.

For Acme, Inc.:   For Summit Consulting Group, Inc.:

_____   _____

Wile E. Coyote   Alan Weiss, PhD President,
Vice President   Predation
Date: March 2, 2012

I'm not going to provide a practice space with this one because you merely use the template above, substituting as necessary.

I send two copies of my proposals in hard copy even if the buyer has requested an electronic version, and I sign all copies before sending them. I don't see the need to have the buyer sign, then I countersign, then I return a copy again. I want speed, not bureaucracy, and since all of this is predicated on a trusting relationship with the buyer, and I'm dealing only with the buyer, there is no danger in signing and sending it along. I use FedEx all the time.

The buyer typically signs one and returns one, or signs one "electronically." But see the case study above where I never did receive the signed contract. I will work on a "telephone handshake," or even an e-mail one, though I prefer a signed document, because:

- Buyers change.
- Others may eventually want to review it.
- It indicates commitment not just to payment terms, but to outcomes, time frames, accountabilities, and so forth.
- If the project is delayed per the allowance in the proposal, it's more important than ever to have documentation for starting up again.
- Lawyers sometimes appear unexpectedly when you open the cellar door by mistake.

The architecture, as I'm calling it, is in these nine clear steps:

1. Situation appraisal
2. Objectives
3. Metrics
4. Value
5. Methodology and options
6. Timing
7. Joint accountabilities
8. Terms and conditions
9. Acceptance

Contrast this to the semi-bound, quasi-legal monstrosities you've seen in so many instances, which provide the unfortunate opportunity for the buyer to quite legitimately claim that he or she requires help from legal, finance, HR, implementers, stakeholders, colleagues, and so on. The more you say, the more you leave yourself open to be second-guessed or discussed.

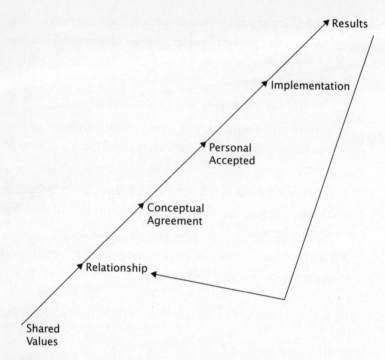

FIGURE 4.1   The consulting business model

The principle from the earlier chapters is what carries the day here: conceptual agreement with a true, economic buyer about objectives, measures of success, and the value of achieving those objectives for the organization and the buyer personally. As you can see in Figure 4.1, the proposal is submitted *after* a lead is qualified, a buyer is found, a relationship is established, and conceptual agreement is obtained. That can be a tough wait for many consultants, but it's the royal road (and even expressway) to high-value proposals being accepted 80 percent of the time or better.

This approach also eliminates the need for personally presenting the proposal, for "dog and pony" shows, and for facing most committees. We'll talk more about that in the next chapter.

You've seen here, if you've completed the few exercises, how readily this sequence can be applied to your own business. So the key point from here is your own discipline and talent, and we turn to those two vital factors now.

Notes

1. The least expensive option must still meet all the project objectives or you're being unethical. The idea is to build value above and beyond the minimum stated in the larger options.

2. You can have two options or seven, but I've found three to provide the best assortment of easy choice and differentiation for the buyer to quickly consider.

3. Noncompete would also go here, but these should be rare and very expensive. See my books *Million Dollar Consulting* (McGraw-Hill) and *Value-Based Fees* (John Wiley & Sons).

4. For example, the buyer finds out that divestiture is in the works, or I find out that three vice presidents have their resumes on the street.

One Dozen Golden Rules for Presenting Proposals

Steak and Sizzle Are Hard to Beat

Speed and Responsiveness

I promise my proposals within 24 hours in almost all cases. (Taking an international flight might prohibit this, but not always.) I can write it on the flight then e-mail it from my laptop or iPad on landing. Since I'd rarely schedule a flight like that the same day as a major meeting, it's rarely ever been a problem, and it's the kind of problem I love if I do have it!

Speed is of the essence. Too many bad things can happen the longer you wait to submit your proposal:

- A client priority radically shifts.
- Unexpected internal and external events intervene.
- The buyer becomes ill or is reassigned or has personal problems.
- A subordinate decides to resist because it's threatening.
- Legal and finance and HR get wind of it, and stick their noses in.
- Across-the-board cuts are made.

You get the idea. Absence does not make the heart grow fonder; it makes people forget. You want to ride the wave of the positives you've created: trust, conceptual agreement, value, excitement. Consequently, you want to instantiate the discussions, ideas, concepts, agreements, and related matters in a formalized way as soon as you possibly can.

I'm suggesting that as soon as you possibly can is the next business day.

Since my proposal "architecture" is really a template, I suggest that you modify it within reason for your needs (e.g., you may want to include something about intellectual property if it worries you, but *never* include resumes for you and your staff), and then simply "plug in" the appropriate content in each of the nine areas.

Once you do that, you can read it through for flow and logic, and then finalize it. As I mentioned in the prior chapter, send two executed copies by FedEx to your buyer's personal attention, and send an electronic copy only if requested.

Glossary

Instantiate: To convert intangibles into pragmatic, clear examples for action and next steps.

Digression: Electronic Proposals

I realize some people request and prefer these, and I'm no Luddite. I'm working as a coauthor right now on a book tentatively titled *Web Dreams*. Having said that, here are my reservations about electronically submitted proposals:

- The formatting is easily scrambled, and small errors can make major differences, as with decimal points, months, and so on.

- They are unsecure, and a secretary or assistant may regularly intercept e-mail (they are less likely to open a personal FedEx), and they may talk to friends in legal or HR.

- E-mail with attachments is often blocked or redirected for security reasons.

- It's far too easy to include someone else's e-mail by accident, either at your end or the client's end.

- You lose the richness of your letterhead, presentation folder, and so forth.

For those reasons, I'll send hard copy no matter what. I'm not using FedEx as a generic here, either. I use Federal Express because it has by far the best service, highest reliability, and easiest tracking. (I remember the DHL guy who would appear in a little van, smoking a cigarette to deliver to me. I don't want his cousin delivering to my clients.)

The proper sequence then, looks something like this:

1. Conclude your conceptual agreement meeting in person with a summary and definitive next steps (see the final segment in this chapter).

2. Write the proposal immediately—if you're back in the office that day, fine, otherwise write it in your travels. Consider allowing time to write it in the city you're visiting before taking the first flight home. Treat yourself to a good meal and celebrate.

3. Review it for accuracy (it helps to have someone else read it for typos) and send it via FedEx. Track the progress. E-mail the client that it's en route, and include the client's e-mail address in the FedEx options for notification for "sent," "exceptions,"[1] and "received." This way, if the buyer should tell you later that it wasn't received, you can specify exactly who signed for it and when. (This has happened to me because internal mail operations don't necessarily assign the best and the brightest there.)

4. Contact the client as established in the next two days.

Three golden rules:

1. Write the proposal rapidly and completely at your first opportunity.

2. Get it to the client by the fastest means,[2] which may include FedEx and electronics.

3. Enable the client and yourself to follow up on its progress.

Before we move on, consider this: The speed and responsiveness demonstrated by your proposal submission is a clear and vivid indication of the speed and responsiveness the client can expect of you during the ensuing project. That is no small matter, no small example to set, and is seldom unnoticed. If you can provide a substantial proposal succinctly and rapidly, the chances are you can fulfill your project obligations in the same manner.

The proposal is the curtain being raised on the project. It's an opportunity for the "audience" to understand what's to follow, and become engaged and absorbed early. In the theater, they often talk about "the front of the house," so that people have a positive experience arriving and the curtain can go up on time.

This is your "front of the house." The important thing is for you to arrive on time! Get the place cleaned up, usher your buyer into the right seat, adjust the lighting, create the right mood, and sell the popcorn!

Accurate Re-creations

The word above is "re-creation," as in formulating again, not what goes on in a rec room! By "re-creation" I mean that you should be faithfully re-creating the conceptual agreement reached with the economic buyer.

This means that you shouldn't be including everything that happens to be stored and accessible on your computer. You should be providing the "bare-bones" essential to keep the buyer on the straight and narrow trail.

Case Study: Heft versus Gravitas

I had received a call from a buyer at a previous client, now at a new firm, to meet with him and submit a proposal for a project. It was a different kind of firm from his prior one, so I believed that I should convince him of my qualifications for that type of business, despite our previous relationship and conceptual agreement achieved during our meeting.

(continued)

> When I called as promised a few days after the proposal submission, he said, "Alan, I'm sorry, but that 'core dump' you did of every visual you've ever created was distracting and leads me to believe you may not be comfortable with this particular type of intervention. Maybe next time."
> There never was a "next time."

Here's what you *don't* want to include in the proposal package and why. Don't even think about it, assuming, of course, that you have conceptual agreement with a buyer in place. If not, then don't just refrain from what's below, refrain from sending a proposal altogether.

- Resumes: These are used to get jobs, not to supply credentials for proposals, especially when you've already met with the buyer. And resumes for your staff are pointless. If the buyer trusts you, shouldn't the buyer trust your judgment about your associates and colleagues?

- Promotional materials: That horse left the barn just before the cows came home. Why on earth attempt to support your credibility now, after successful buyer interactions?

- Deliverables: HR is famous for requesting "deliverables" because HR people seem incapable of thinking about outcomes. Whatever tasks or interventions you'll be performing can be lightly covered in the "options and methodology" section of the proposal.

- Charts and graphs: These are seldom useful at this juncture because you already have agreement, and they can tend to cause reservations if they are misunderstood or

---

Glossary

Cover letter: The introduction to the proposal that contains certain promises, agreements, and expectations that accompany and are inherent in the proposal.

---

are shared with others who have not been privy to the prior conversations.

- Gifts or incentives: Don't even suggest that there is some lagniappe involved, even a brochure to a college the buyer's daughter is considering. The only incentive should be the early payment discount, which profits the entire organization.

If those are items that should not be included—which is why 2.5 pages is usually totally sufficient—what else should be included?

Put the proposal in your best presentation folder along with a cover letter. Here is a sample cover letter.

March 3, 2012

Wile E. Coyote
Vice President, Predation
Acme Co., Inc.
85 Canyon Dr.
Notsocarefree, AZ 88901

Dear Wile,
As promised, I've enclosed two copies of the proposal reflecting our agreements reached yesterday in your office. I've forwarded an electronic version as well this morning.

(continued)

Please choose the option you prefer, the payment terms you prefer, and return one of the copies I've already signed via the FedEx envelope enclosed. I've also enclosed an invoice in different varieties in case this helps in the process.

I'm prepared to begin within a week of your acceptance, as discussed.

Please note that this proposal is copyrighted and contains my intellectual property. It may not be shared with anyone outside of your organization for any reason without my express approval.

I'll call you Friday at 10 A.M. as agreed, if I don't hear from you prior, to see which choices you've made. If you'd like to begin immediately with a telephone "handshake," I'm happy to accommodate you.

Thanks for the opportunity to work with you on this important project.

Sincerely,
Alan Weiss, PhD
President

Note that you're stressing that this may not be shown to competitors, the exact date and time of your follow-up, there is a FedEx envelope with your account number enclosed, and there are invoices to expedite the initial payments.

You've also allowed for an immediate start on the basis of a phone call. When the client does accept, either with a signature or a call, try to begin right away, on-site. This "pours cement" on the agreement. Even if you have other client engagements, you can always work in a brief visit to make some observations and conduct some interviews.

Let's explore why you don't need more pitch and promotion, just to ensure that you're comfortable. So forget all the resumes and jive. But make sure that cover letter is firmly attached and writ large!

Three golden rules:

  4. Leave out as much as you can.

  5. Ensure that the hard copy looks great.

  6. Don't mistake the proposal for promotion.

Counterintuitive: No Pitch or Promotion

I'm a devotee of the television phenomenon *American Idol*. One of the most hackneyed and trite critiques of the singers offered by the judges—especially Randy Jackson, who's become known for it—is "pitchy." In singing, this means that one is out of the proper tonal range, which can be caused by not hearing yourself, or by nerves, or simply by singing too loudly (which often results from the first two conditions).

You can also be too "pitchy" in your proposal, and it may seem counterintuitive to many of you that this is such a "low key," explanatory document. So first I'll reiterate: *A proposal is a summation, not an exploration, and not a negotiation.* This is not a debating document, thus it needn't make points about *why* the buyer should pursue this. We already know that from prior discussions. This is rather about *how* the buyer should do this (hence, the options I insist upon presenting).

The more you provide a "take it or leave it" approach, the more you're faced with a "hard sell." An auto showroom with a single model is going to have some hard-pressed salespeople, but one with 20 models has salespeople who say, "If you're looking for better mileage, just step over here," or "If it's something sportier that makes sense, let's walk out onto the lot."

Under the best of conditions, a binary decision (do it or don't do it) will give you a 50/50 chance. I'm not commenting on how well you've set it up, merely that there are two possible outcomes (despite the fact that the decision may be made immediately or delayed). With three options, however, you have no, yes, yes, and yes. You now have four possible outcomes, of which three are favorable, even though they differ in degree. (A project with the lowest option is far superior to no project at all.)

As options increase, however, the advantage disappears. Again, this may sound counterintuitive, but consider this: With the advent of the proliferation of investment and retirement vehicles in an increasingly turbulent and unpredictable global economy, fewer people actually decide on even attractive alternatives and simply allow their money to sit in low (e.g., 1 percent or less) savings accounts. People walking into television stores find themselves faced with flat-screen, different sizes, 3-D, projection, home theater, surround sound, digital light processing, liquid crystal display, rear projection, and so on. And as a result, they often leave the store without deciding, whereas a decade ago the choice was simple and immediately made.

What's needed isn't a "pitch" but a set of optimal choices all focused on a yes of some kind. My experience concludes that this is three, but you may deem four or two your preference. My analysis looks like this:

Option	Percentage of Times Chosen
1	15%
2	60%
3	25%

As they say in the TV ads, "under actual conditions your results may vary"! However, these are the results of my own work and thousands of people who have mentored with me. This means that when a proposal is accepted, a quarter of the time the top and most expensive option is selected, and *85 percent of the time one of the top two is selected.* That is a huge increase in your annual income because, if you don't provide options but rather a single choice, that fee is usually somewhere between Options 1 and 2.

You'd be leaving (and maybe have already left) a great deal of money on the table.

In my experience, about 80 percent of value-based proposals—following a trusting relationship and conceptual agreement with an economic buyer—are accepted. Some of my mentees have reported acceptance consistently in the 90 percent range. But let's remain conservative.

If your average proposal options are for $50,000, $70,000, and $90,000 and you submit two per month, that's 24 proposals a year, of which 19 would be accepted. Of the 19, three would produce $150,000 (Option 1); 11 would produce $770,000 (Option 2); and five would produce $450,000 (Option 3). That's a total of $1,370,000 without a single proposal's option in six figures, yet many of you do and should be bidding six figures for a great deal of your work.

If you were providing the single option, between the points I mentioned is usually the case (between Options 1 and 2), that amount would have been $60,000 times 19 projects, or $1,140,000, *which represents a quarter million dollars left on the table.* However, what's not included in my calculations is that the single-option, take-it-or-leave-it proposal would *not* close at a rate of 80 percent. Let's be kind and say that your closing rate is better than 50/50—call it 65 percent. That means 16 proposals close at $60,000 each, which is $960,000, or $410,000 less than the approach with three options and a higher close rate, which is *a 30 percent decline in potential income.*

Over the course of five years, that grows to about $2 million. If your proposals tend to be less than the average or more than the average above, simply adjust the figures accordingly. But the fact is that you are leaving money on the table each year, which *you will never be able to recover.* It's gone. And it was all bottom-line profit. Over a decade that's the difference between comfortable retirement and forced work; between being able to take prudent risk and having to be archly conservative; between philanthropy and penuriousness.

Try this out, just to personalize the impact, by using your last full year's results:

Number of Proposals Submitted	Accepted	%	Total Fees	Average Fee

Now apply my averages, assuming that you had an option 15 percent below your average fee (1), 15 percent above it (2), and 25 percent above it (3). Apply the percentages above to your close rate and the options that would have been accepted:

Submitted:_____ Accepted at 80%:_____

Avg. Rates for: Option 1 $____   Option 2 $____   Option 3 $____

Numbers accepted at: Option 1 (15%): ____   Option 2 (60%) ____   Option 3 (25%) ____

Rate for Option # X # accepted: Option 1 $____   Option 2 $____   Option 3 $____

Actual income from proposals last year: $_____   With this system: $_____

Difference: $_____

What differences do you see? Is it worth thinking about following the simple, disciplined system, and worrying less about pitch and more about process? How much money did you leave on the table last year?

Three golden rules:

7. Options escalate business dramatically.

8. If you don't ask, you don't get.

9. You are past the point of return in terms of negotiating.

To Be or Not to Be (In Person)

It's a bad idea to deliver a completed proposal in person.

I know that flies in the face of what you've been told, what you do, and even a positive experience or two you've had, but it's an overwhelmingly bad idea.

Now I guess you're going to want to know why.

- Timing: This delays receipt and acceptance. You have to produce a convenient date for you and the buyer, which could take a week or a month. If something emerges in the interim or during that meeting requiring an adjustment, then the delay becomes even longer.

- Temperature: You allow the process to cool down considerably. The next day (which is why I've advocated speed and FedEx or electronics) the buyer is still enthused, very conversant, and convinced. As the days grow long you reach the December of the (northern hemisphere) year: cool and icy conditions.

- Intermezzo: Restaurants often provide an intermezzo, or palate cleaner, between courses, to remove prior tastes. You don't want that course served here. Too many interferences can surface that neither you nor the buyer had anticipated (or had anticipated as much less of an issue) the longer you take to get there.

- Crowds: There is at least an odds-on chance that, because you're coming back to present the proposal, the buyer will invite in (or others will inveigle in) random colleagues and subordinates, who may well pose objections and resistance the buyer had underestimated. It's unlikely that the buyer would invite this cabal to review a written proposal received the next day after your meeting.

- Production: It's often assumed that the presentation of a proposal requires PowerPoint, handouts, models, and at least three trained seals. Why are you there with merely a 2.5-page proposal that is totally clear and crisp?

- Questions: As long as you're there, the buyer is going to utilize the time to explore every nook and cranny. There will be minor questions that become major pains, semicolons that require more than a short pause, and suggestions for amendments and redaction.

- Negotiation: It's much tougher in person than on the phone for most consultants to steel themselves to reject requests for fee compromise. When the buyer says, "I love Option 3, but the price is a tad high," on the phone you can reply, "That's why we have Option two!" But sitting on a couch, drinking coffee, with the buyer smiling and winking, how steeled are you going to be? After all, *if this isn't a negotiating document, then why have you returned in person to discuss it at all?*

And there is the rub.

Once you show up, especially after more than a couple of days—and it's often more than a month in many instances, given travel and other priorities for both parties—the dynamics have changed. There are new priorities, views from precincts not reporting in previously, less intimate familiarity with the details, less fervor about and belief in the ROI.

Your proposal is copyrighted, and you've stipulated within it that it's not to be shown to anyone outside of the organization—thereby preventing, one hopes, the sharing of contents with competing consultants. But on top of all of that, you have a trusting relationship with the buyer.

Therefore, your written proposal should be sufficient for you to place before the buyer without the potential negatives of setting up and conducting a personal meeting for discussion and acceptance. And don't forget this:

- Returns: Any changes, additions, or deletions agreed on in a personal meeting must be changed, usually through more than a hand notation but rather with a new, altered proposal, which will take more of your time to create and return and have accepted. And the buyer just may suggest that you return in person for a "final" discussion with the amendments.

Digression About Trust

When a buyer says, "Great proposal, it's made it to the short list," or "We're now looking only at you and one other firm," or "Someone else is 25 percent less expensive making it a harder choice for me," you do not have a trusting relationship with the buyer.

The relationship you develop, coupled with conceptual agreement with its inherent ROI, should place you in a completely different category from competitors. Hence, the time required to develop that relationship actually results in faster, higher quality business.

If I—as an economic buyer—trust you and believe in the goals we've mutually established, then someone else's lower price isn't going to be even a vague issue. Don't rush the proposal creation, but do rush its delivery.

- Expense: The client isn't going to be paying your expenses in 98 percent of these excursions, so that you may be spending thousands, which reduce the margin of the project by increasing acquisition costs considerably. The idea is to *reduce* acquisitions costs! (And if you aren't successful in obtaining the project—which in best cases will be at least 20 percent of the time—you're incurring tens of thousands in unnecessary reductions to your bottom line annually.)

So, to be or not to be?

Not.

Near the end of this famous Shakespearean soliloquy, Hamlet observes:

> *With this regard their currents turn awry,*
> *And lose the name of action.*

You don't want to "lose the name of action." You're going to accelerate the process (or at least maintain the current velocity) ironically by staying away. Educate the client about this near the end of your conceptual agreement meeting. "If we're agreed, I'll summarize this in a brief proposal, get it to you tomorrow, and call you Friday at 10 for your choice of options and terms. There's no need to take up any more of your time until then."

So let's turn to Friday at 10, when you *do* need to "show up."

Two golden rules:

10. You're most influential when you're not there with the proposal.

11. Don't fix things that are working just fine.

Definitive Dates and Times

A discipline that's key to our professional lives is especially salient in terms of proposals. I call them "sedulous next steps," or SNS.

Nowhere is a definitive future, agreed-upon action more important than in developing, documenting, and delivering proposals. It's rather useless to promise a proposal quickly and then take your time following up. Speed and milestones are as important as detail and description.

Before you leave the buyer and after the conceptual agreement, you should use language such as this:

> *I'll have this on your desk before 10:30 on Thursday. Are you available Friday afternoon at 2 to chat by phone so that I can find out your choices?*
>
> *If not, what time is best on Monday? Would you prefer I call your cell phone or office number?*

If you have a conceptual agreement based on a trusting relationship, you should *not* receive a response such as:

- I'll get back to you when I can next week.
- Call me in about two weeks.
- I'll need to have some of my people review what you send.
- Take your time, there is no rush here.
- Why don't you schedule another meeting and bring it by?

All of these are "stop" signs requiring that you return, like Groundhog Day, to an earlier part of the conversation and reestablish (or establish for the first time) a trusting relationship, value, a sense of urgency, and definitive next steps. A failure to do this is why so many consultants complain to me that, "I can't understand it, the buyer won't return my calls despite our productive meeting."

Productive for whom?

Here is a typical schedule you can follow and even place in your briefcase to refer to during your visit:

Step	When
1. Establish conceptual agreement	During meeting with economic buyer *after trust is established*[3]
2. Reconfirm conceptual agreement	Prior to end of meeting
3. Set time and date for buyer to expect proposal	Prior to end of meeting
4. Set time and date for follow-up after proposal is received	Prior to end of meeting
5. Set contingency time and date in case follow-up is missed	Prior to end of meeting

Thus:

> *I'll have this on your desk before 10:30 on Thursday. Are you available Friday afternoon at 2 to chat by phone so that I can find out your choices?*
>
> *If not, what time is best on Monday? Would you prefer I call your cell phone or office number? In case something occurs that we don't anticipate and we miss that call, how is Monday morning before the day begins, say at 8:45?*

We've covered why the buyer might not be responsive when you don't create SNS (e.g., the buyer just wants you to be gone and really hasn't felt a trusting relationship grow). But why would

Glossary

SNS: Sedulous next steps are those vital connections between you and the buyer, which maintain momentum and minimize time duration. They are important throughout the marketing and delivery relationships, but absolutely critical in the proposal stage.

the buyer not respond if you *do* have a trusting relationship and tight conceptual agreement?

- Personal concerns have arisen that trump all else
- Illness
- Emergency assignment
- Company emergency (e.g., lawsuit)
- Interference and interruption by others/shifting priorities
- "Cools off" to the value after you leave
- Learns new, pertinent information that's discouraging
- Misses or misplaces your call/forgets

For these and allied reasons, I've been suggesting the following preventive and contingent actions:

- Take your time to gain trust and test that trust, for example, is the buyer sharing with you and seeking advice?
- Reconfirm everything on the spot, while you're there.
- Set definitive next times and dates.
- Set contingency times and dates.
- Request a cell phone number and/or personal e-mail.
- Ask while together, "Are there any obstacles you can conceive which might delay your acceptance of my proposal that we haven't yet discussed?"[4]

- Move quickly—as quickly as you can. This is enhanced by our very brief and pithy proposal format.
- Ask the buyer's secretary or assistant if anything is preventing a return call if the original and contingency aren't made.
- Don't assume the buyer is damaged or dishonest or uninterested.
- These judgments will adversely affect your behavior.
- Make three calls, and then write a hard copy letter. We'll talk about this contingency more a bit later.

Understand for now that time is money in the sense that the faster you are, the more you'll make. But let's look at adverse events that occur despite your best plans.

One golden rule:

12. Get there firstest with the mostest and measure it with your calendar.

Notes

1. This enables the buyer and you to be told that FedEx had a mechanical problem or a storm cancelled the flight.
2. Which *is not* in person, and which I discuss later in the chapter.
3. This may take more than one meeting in certain circumstances, so be sure to schedule the next meeting while you're there.
4. If the buyer says, "Yes, I haven't seen your fees!" respond, "That's true, and you'll see fees, options, and ROI in detail tomorrow!"

Why Bad Things Happen to Good People Who Wait

Moving Mountains

How and When to Follow Up

As we've discussed, you follow up quickly on an agreed-upon date at an agreed-upon time. If you reach voice mail or an assistant, you simply say, "I'm calling as promised." If you have a trusting relationship, the buyer should have you on the calendar and take your call. If the buyer has encountered an unavoidable conflict, then the buyer should call you back promptly.

That's the best of all possible worlds, a Candidian outcome. Your inquiry should then be an assumptive closing statement, such as:

> *Which option have you decided to implement?*
> *Which payment option do you prefer?[1]*

If for any reason you have not set a definitive time and date with the buyer, then my advice is to contact the buyer 24 hours after receipt of the proposal. If you're using FedEx you can track that and actually see who signed for it and when (anticipating the possible reaction, "Did we get it?"). Always do this by phone, never e-mail. Consultants are afraid to use the phone, I think because the possible rejection is starker than by e-mail. Get rid of that mind-set. Pick up the phone and call.

My general rule for any unreturned communications is three tries and a letter. That means that after three calls, you send a hard copy letter (avoid getting lost in e-mail) and say the following:

> I'm sorry we couldn't make contact. I'm here if you need me, but I certainly don't want to hound you. After three attempts, I'm respecting your privacy but am happy to continue when you're ready.

When people don't get back to you it's not because they're busy, it's because they're rude and unprofessional. (This is much more common at lower levels and within HR than with executives, by the way, who have no need to create artificial power in this manner by being nonresponsive.) It's passive/aggressive behavior that is detestable, so don't throw good time and money after bad. However, you needn't burn bridges. My two lines above are polite and leave the bridge intact.

It's always a good idea to cultivate a relationship with the buyer's secretary, assistant, or key subordinate during your visits if possible. You can then call them and say:

> I need your advice. Is she in town and, if so, what's the best time to reach her? Can you put me on her calendar?

The old bromide works well here: Call early in the morning or after hours. Many buyers are at their desk by 8 and still there at 6, with their line open because their assistant isn't there and they may be expecting calls (though not yours!).

If the buyer does take the call as planned, and responds, "Option 2, we'll send the 50 percent deposit tomorrow, when can you start?" then simply move forward. You may say:

> *Thank you, I'm looking forward to our partnership. Will you use the invoice and FedEx envelope I enclosed, or will you need something else? (Some firms need to give you an accounts payable number or require proof of malpractice insurance coverage, and so forth.) While I have you on the phone, let's get everything squared away. How is Tuesday morning to start? Can you and I meet for 30 minutes?*

If at some later time, accounts payable or a similar function has someone contact you to inform you that the provisions of your proposal are out of policy, or that they intend to pay you 60 days, net, or that you'll have to jump through other hoops, simply go back to your buyer and emphasize the terms and conditions that were accepted in your proposal. Don't argue with bureaucrats, that's all they have to do. Let your buyer do the heavy lifting.

Some firms (especially overseas) will want to wire funds. Make sure that they have your international routing (SWIFT) number, your account name and number, your bank's name and address, and a management contact at the bank. In my experience, wired funds take from 3 to 10 days to reach your account once initiated by the client.

Do not accept foreign currency checks, no checks in U.S. funds drawn on a non-U.S. bank. The bank will return it, *via normal mail,* to get their exchange and will charge you a fee for taking so long to do it. U.S. funds must be drawn on a U.S. bank. Most foreign banks have U.S. counterpart relationships.

> ## Case Study: Purchasing Problem
>
> After I had reached a deal with Tom, the general manager, I was to start in two weeks. In the interim, Peggy called me from purchasing to inform me that Tom "wasn't authorized" to conduct negotiations with "vendors."
>
> "I'm a consultant, not a vendor," I pointed out.
>
> "You're a vendor to me," she sniffed. Then she told me that I was to provide an hourly rate, and if it was more than 10 times higher than the average of the last six consultants who worked there, I would have to lower it.
>
> "You'll do that or you won't work here," she said.
>
> "Good-bye," I said.
>
> I called Tom and he told me he had heard about such things, and that he'd take care of it.
>
> He had Peggy fired. I have no remorse. Her job was to support the line executives, not to play traffic cop. I realized that arguing with her was a losing proposition, and that I had no intention of losing in the end.

Accept credit cards when the client requests it. The fees you'll have to pay (generally from 2 to 3.5 percent) are a cost of doing business. On a $30,000 fee, that's about $900, which is worth it to get the money in your account quickly.

In most cases, you'll get through to your buyer and he or she will choose an option to proceed. Life being what it is, other things can occur. So let's take a look at what you can reasonably anticipate getting in the way and how to cope.

What to Anticipate and How to Cope

I mentioned earlier that my "hit rate" with this process is about 80 percent, though some people in my Mentor Program report upward of 90 percent. In any case, that means that about 60 percent of the time I simply get a yes, 20 percent I have to cope with "issues," and 20 percent I simply don't get the business.[2]

Bad things happen to good people like you and often me. You can anticipate some and cope with them or even resolve them.

1. The client loves an Option 3 facet but cannot approve expenditures above Option 2.

In this case, technically there is another buyer just for Option 3, because you've exceeded your buyer's grant of authority with it. But it makes no sense to try to move to that more senior person when your buyer is ready to proceed. Nor does it make sense here to cavalierly say (as I often do suggest to those buyers who have the money but want to see if they can get a "deal"), "Well, that's why we have Option 2."

You can't just grant Option 3 at Option 2 fees because the next question is, "How low will you go?" Perhaps to Option 1 prices?

But what you can do is to move things around. Suggest that you can move one facet from 3 to 2 at a slightly higher price or, if possible in the context of your options, take some things out of 2, move something from 3 in, and simply charge the Option 2 fee. It helps to be flexible in these cases if you believe your buyer simply doesn't have the ability to invest more. But you must show that you're removing something, not just lowering the fee.

2. The client can't approve a check over a certain amount even though the buyer has a budget for more than the total amount.

It's often the case that the buyer has a $500,000 budget, for example, but can't approve checks over $150,000 without another officer's approval or a committee review. That can be deadly, because people without any interest in or appreciation of the project will feel it their earthly calling to question the amount being invested.

The best way to cope with this is to suggest that the buyer authorize more than one check at his or her grant of authority until the full amount is paid. This may require that you change the terms of payment or that time frames be extended or work protocols shifted. You'll find a case study earlier in the book where this exact issue arose and was handled in this manner.

You do not want your proposals going to the legal department or to executives who have not participated in the process. So suggest this alternative to your buyer. (Many will suggest it to you.)

3. Your buyer says something to others that threatens the project.

Rehearse with your buyer if for any reason other high-level people need to be apprised of the work that's to come prior to the proposal being signed. I'm not talking about further approvals, which means that you haven't been speaking to the real buyer. But often there are executive councils or senior committees of which your buyer is a member and on a regular basis they inform each other of changes in their operations so that others can copy best practices or adjust to new ones (which is actually a pretty good idea).

But your client should not mention details of the proposal, merely the results expected of a new initiative. Ideally, the buyer shouldn't even mention you. But coach the buyer: For example, tell the buyer asked about the cost to simply say the proposal hasn't been reviewed yet although it should clearly be well within budget. This will help you avoid an inadvertent creation of some other interested but unhelpful parties.

4. The buyer gets cold feet.

This is the reason that I urge you to act speedily and with all due haste. You want to strike while the buyer is still warm in the glow of your agreement. But, stuff happens.

The causes can be legion, and we'll deal with legitimate, last-minute objections below. They can include an unexpected event, a random comment by a superior, fear expressed by a subordinate, even a misunderstanding by you or the buyer that emerges when the buyer sees everything in writing.

Case Study: The Careless Comment

One of my Mentor Program Members in a European country had the equivalent of a $2 million project approved by the COO, who had budget and responsibility for such things. However, before it was signed, a board meeting was scheduled and the executive had to appear and report on new developments. He invited my colleague to observe the meeting as a courtesy.

This particular board included two members of the union, per the contract. At the conclusion of the COO's report, another board member casually asked what the price was, and the COO told him. The two union members immediately came to attention and suggested strongly that the matter be studied, given the immensity of the fee. The chair had no choice but to agree.

My colleague was told two days later that the project was dead. For all of his preparation, he had never rehearsed with his buyer what to say if asked about the fee.

Follow up your proposal quickly. If you sense *any* hesitancy, confront it at the time, not later. In other words, if the buyer says, "I looked it over and things seem just as we agreed, but I'd like to. . ." then ask immediately why he or she feels it necessary to talk to others, to take a few more days, to compare it to the strategic plan, and so forth—whatever it is that finishes that sentence above. Don't hesitate.

Before you leave the buyer with conceptual agreement attained, always ask, "Is there anything you can think of that would be an obstacle to us working together once you see the proposal and the investment levels provide for dramatic return?" Try to ferret out what you can at that point. But if you encounter this when you make your follow-up call, confront it: "I'm not sure why that would help in any way, and I'm concerned that you may see obstacles that we hadn't discussed. Please tell me what, specifically, gives you cause for pause at this point?"

Don't be afraid to do this. The longer the buyer takes, the more bad things can happen. The faster the decision, the faster the best thing happens.

Overcoming Last-Minute Objections

There are legitimate objections that arise at the last moment, along with not-so-legitimate ones. There really are no objections you haven't heard before, so it's negligent not to be ready for all of them. You may not win every battle, but you should give a good fight.

Last-minute objections fall into these four categories:

1. Genuine misunderstandings.
2. Legitimate intervening events.
3. Resistance encountered from others.
4. Illegitimate fears.

1. Genuine Misunderstandings

The buyer may have said that sales could be improved by 15 percent, but the client meant over two years and you thought it was over a single year. Hence, the returns may seem overly optimistic in your proposal. Or you may have said that your company would run all focus groups (meaning subcontractors or employees you routinely utilize) but the buyer thought that you, personally, would conduct them all. These things happen in all business meetings and there is no malice or incompetence involved (unless they *repeatedly* happen to you).

The cure here is to ask the buyer what would make him or her happy, and see if you can accommodate that. Compromises are fine. You want to try to avoid lowering fees. For example, lowering the return to the first two years rather than the first year is not so debilitating, and may mean a 14:1 return on investment the first year instead of 20:1, which is still impressive. And it may be possible for you to agree to do half the focus groups or personally conduct interviews or convince the client that your people are better at focus groups than you are, which is why you have them conduct the sessions. No harm done.

Take the responsibility for all misunderstandings, whether your fault or not, and try to preserve your fees by offering compromises or showing the buyer that there's nothing to fear.

2. Legitimate Intervening Events

A company plant blows up. (It's happened to me.) The buyer's boss is fired, or replaced, or leaves on extended disability. There is a purchase or divestiture announced. A company employee is kidnapped overseas. There is a major technology crash. A competitor gains a huge leap.

These things happen regularly, so the odds are that they will happen in between the submission of your proposal and its acceptance at some points in your career. Be prepared.

My recommendations:

- If you hear through other channels, phone your buyer immediately. If your buyer tells you, then suggest that you immediately confront the issue.
- My favored alternative is to suggest that the causes and reasons for the project haven't actually been changed by anything that has transpired. So there really is no good reason to stop, just as there is no reason for the organization to suddenly stop doing business.
- If the change is too severe for the project to persevere, suggest to the client that you reorient your work within

the budget of the first proposal (and options) to help with the issue at hand. The buyer has designated time, money, and you, so why not capitalize on those resources to attack the new challenge?

• If the first two don't work, force the buyer to agree to a specific date to talk again to review the status. Remind the buyer that the current terms and conditions are good for 90 days only. (Some consultants actually put time deadlines in their proposals. I don't because I want to encourage clients to act *immediately* and not believe they have a 90-day window.)

3. Resistance Encountered From Others

On many occasions, others will know of the pending project and proposal. Monies may have been budgeted, people's opinions sought, a gaggle of consultants brought in, and so forth. Some of those people want to undermine proposals because they are threatened by the intervention.

The best preventive action for this is to apprise your buyer in advance of this likelihood. (This is especially important if you're asked to chat with subordinates by the client.) Tell the buyer that people tend to be threatened or offended that they aren't called to take the lead internally on such projects.

If the resistance still arises, suggest to the client that there are two options:

1. Co-opt the resistance. The buyer can talk to those involved and ensure them a role (and credit) in the implementation aspect.

2. Overwhelm the resistance. Tell them it's a *fait accompli* and they had better get used to it, because they're all expected to float on this boat.

Finally, point out that the decision is strategic, appropriate for the buyer, but not for people who are the tacticians and implementers. Sometimes tough decisions are required to effect the greatest positive change.

4. Illegitimate Fears

Your buyer and those around him may fear the following:

- The unknown
- Failure
- Embarrassment
- Bruised egos
- Significant change
- Going "public" with a new initiative
- Risk
- Fear itself

Fears aren't uncommon, but these I call "illegitimate" because they really shouldn't derail a significant buyer oriented toward improving his or her operation. The recipe for dealing with this is simple: Isolate the actual fear from my list above (it's not *all* of these, after all); then ask what is the worst that can happen; demonstrate that you have preventive actions in place as well as contingencies; and point out that any new venture entails some degree of acceptable risk.

So if embarrassment is the issue, demonstrate that continued performance at the current level without any visible attempts at improvement is much more embarrassing, and that even modest improvement would look very good, and that the two of you are prepared to handle whatever arises through additional training or a slower pace (the benefit of value-based fees).

It's darkest just before the dawn.

Overcoming Legitimate Obstacles

There are legitimate obstacles that arise even at this late juncture, which is why "hit rates" aren't even higher with this system. But you can maximize your rate of acceptance if you prepare for the common causes of last-minute interference.

Obstacle 1: The buyer is called away.

There have been more occasions than I thought possible in the realm of probability where my buyer has suddenly "vanished." There's an emergency in Puerto Rico and the buyer must rush to San Juan. There's a sudden vacancy in the executive ranks, which the buyer must fill. There's a potential client defection and the buyer must hurry to shore up the relationship.

Personally, the buyer is called away by illness in the family, a birth, a death, an accident, and so forth.

You certainly don't want to intrude in a moment of grief or even celebration, but you do want to be resolute on lesser business issues that suddenly impose themselves. Consequently, here's what to do when you achieve conceptual agreement in person and before you begin to write the proposal.

- Inform the client that sometimes *either of you* can be suddenly co-opted.
- Suggest that you therefore exchange private cell phone numbers and e-mail addresses if you already haven't.
- Agree that a backup plan will be to talk in the evening or on a weekend should a sudden unforeseen issue arise.

Then follow up quickly as I've recommended throughout the book before bad things begin to happen to good people who wait.

Obstacle 2: The buyer's boss becomes involved.

In large organizations, most of your quite legitimate buyers will have quite legitimate superiors. (In small businesses, you'll find the owner often "reports" to a spouse.) Even though the superior need not provide approval or budget, there are times when your buyer may deem it politically correct to mention the project.

This becomes a problem because none of the underlying value has been established with the superior, and you have *no relationship or credibility with the superior*. In larger projects, the buyer's boss may reasonably say, "That's a substantial investment. Are you sure it's the best approach?" And with that simple, reasonable question, the buyer may say, "I do, but if you have other ideas. . ." out of a sense of primal survival need.

In the light of such a possibility:

- Ask the buyer if any of his or her superiors need to be apprised or involved prior to sending the proposal. Offer to meet with them at any time.

- Suggest to the buyer that the contents of the proposal are heavily dependent on the intimate understanding and collaboration achieved by the two of you, and others may not appreciate the value and ROI but merely look at price.

- Ask if there is anything at all you can do to help with internal acceptance if that's an issue.

- After the fact, urge the buyer to introduce you to any inquiring parties because "It's unfair for you to market my abilities and approaches, and I can't allow you to be in such an awkward position."

Obstacle 3: The buyer and/or you have erred.

Sometimes the buyer has believed that some assumptions are facts (i.e., turnover rates or average sales amounts). Sometimes you will be in error on your projections (the percentage increase in sales expected will be only in two areas, not all five). These errors are discovered after the buyer reads the actual proposal, which is really why you've submitted it and the buyer is reading it!

At this point it may seem obvious to merely correct the errors and resubmit the proposal, and that is what you would do. However, you may be doing so with far less value than originally estimated and therefore less ROI, consequently too high a fee. So here are ways to avoid those unpleasantries in case their ugly heads arise:

- Always maximize the value statements from any one objective. Example: The simple objective to increase profits could generate impact (value) including increased investor attraction, better retention of top talent, higher investment in R&D, and larger bonuses.

- Stress that you're taking *the low end of the range* of possible value, or cutting estimates in half. Be very conservative, to demonstrate that there is the potential for much more.

- Maximize the number of objectives in the proposal, which may include revenue, profit, stress reduction, higher visibility, more productivity, less cost, and so on.

- Ensure that you have three solid options, the least of which provides strong value.

- Stress in objectives and value the personal, emotional impact that will be achieved for the buyer.

In providing for these elements, you can go back to the buyer after errors are discovered and point out that there is still huge value and ROI; that a lesser option may now make sense; that the errors are inconsequential; and so forth. You don't want to have to rewrite your proposal but merely have the buyer see that the return may be 12:1 instead of 17:1, or that the emotional gains are still quite present, and that there's no point in making any revisions.

"Bad" things can happen, often suddenly, but their simple occurrence shouldn't be cause for despair or to give up the ship. Some, as you can see, are preventable if you take the right actions early. Others can be dealt with on a contingent basis if they do occur. But the key is that there are things to do, actions to put in place that can minimize this not infrequent stalling point.

It's a shame to have proceeded this far only to let anything less than a natural disaster get in the way of the value you're capable of delivering to your client. Hence, it's incumbent on you to deal with the rapids that sometimes abruptly appear downstream.

Creating a Signature (or Something Else)

The point of all this planning and preparation is to get a signature on the bottom line of the proposal (my ninth category, "Acceptance"), because my proposal format includes the buyer's acceptance and there is no legal contract beyond this document (we'll talk about legal documents and departments in the next chapter).

So how will that happen?

The most basic and fastest route is for the buyer to choose the desired option, sign and date one copy of the proposal, and return it. This is why the two copies I send are *both* executed by me. I don't want the buyer to sign, then return it for me to sign, then return it to the buyer again. Too much time, too much potential for bad things to happen to good people who wait. I also include a FedEx letter envelope already addressed to me by using my account, and an invoice that can be used for any of the options and/or for full payment discount and "normal" 50 percent deposit.

The invoice would look like the one shown in Figure 6.1. You'll note that this can be hard copy or electronic, and I send them in both forms. My federal ID number is on the invoice because many company payment departments demand it, and I don't want them to have to contact me (usually in 30 days!). Also, it's called "Invoice and Statement" because some firms demand one or the other, so I'm covering all bets with a single document.

Specify the funds if you're billing a nondomestic firm or wire instructions.

Box 1009

East Greenwich, RI

0281-0964

Tel (401) 884-2778

Fax (401) 884-5068

INVOICE AND STATEMENT

Date: March 3, 2012   **No. 15398**

For the option chosen in our proposal dated March 2, 2012 and indicated below, per agreement.

Option	50% Deposit	Full Payment Discount
___ #1: $88,000	$44,000	$79,200
___ #2: $109,000	$54,500	$98,100
___ #3: $121,000	$60,500	$108,900

Total Due and Submitted Herein: $_____

Terms: Due upon receipt

Thank You!

Ron Jackson

Vice President, Predation

The Acme Co.

201 Scorch Blvd.

Noncarefree, AZ 00911

Our Federal ID number is 22-2458120

FIGURE 6.1 Invoice and Statement

You may also provide directions for wire transfer or credit card payments, depending on the situation. I tend not to provide these unless the client has requested them, because credit card payments entail interest charges on your part (3 percent on $121,000 is $3,640, for example, and wire transfers also result in a bank charge to you; both modes require up to a week before the deposit clears). If the client needs these alternative payment As it is, checks take a few days a domestic bank involve long

s the proposal copy that will nd payment terms, fills in the the three items in your FedEx ext day.

so easy.

appens, "I want to begin, but ," you don't have an inconve-, any buyer can have a "manual computer check that pops out days" means that your invoice rocurement or accounts payable

best we can do, I'll plan to start eal, and if you've managed to "consultant up" and be a peer of the buyer to this point, don't cave now. You're partners, not buyer/seller. The buyer will usually say, "Let me make a call."

Attack any issues like this as partners: How do *we* resolve this?

Having said that, there are times when you want to begin immediately so the hastening of a signature or reasonable facsimile is important.

For example, the buyer may well call you or respond when you call the buyer a day or so later, "I love this, Option 2 it is, and we have a rare chance to involve all of my country managers at once because they're here this Friday for a conference. Can you come in to meet them and get acquainted? It will help tremendously when you have to talk across long distances later."

The answer to this is, "Of course," as long as your schedule actually permits it.[3] I call this "pouring cement on the sale," because once you're on-site working there is virtually never a retreat on the buyer's part. You simply add, "The proposal calls for payment on commencement, and this is quicker than either of us anticipated, but I'm happy to help. Can you expedite the payment?"

A "telephone handshake" is always good enough for me. If the buyer says, "Go," I start moving. Don't forget that the Acceptance aspect of the proposal says, in effect, "your payment is as good as your signature." So if you get the check, simply ascertain which option, which you should readily tell by the amount, and get cracking.

The beauty of a true economic buyer with a trusting relationship is that his or her word is golden. So start mining. Otherwise, you're going to meet the lawyers.

Notes

1. You don't negotiate terms if you can help it, but there is the option for full payment on acceptance and a 10 percent discount.

2. For those interested, of the 80 percent accepted, Option 1 is taken 25 percent of the time, Option 2 about 25 percent, and Option 3 about 50 percent.

3. If you can't make it, ask about Thursday or even Saturday. These people wouldn't be brought together for a single day, and your buyer may have simply chosen the best time for his or her schedule, but it probably could be altered.

First, Let's Kill All the Lawyers

Shakespeare Really Meant That We Needed Them

Dealing With the Legal Department

Dick Butcher makes the famous comment captured in this chapter title in *Henry VI*, and it's almost always misconstrued. Shakespeare was saying that we need them to keep us honest and killing them is like killing the messenger. (Of course, that was half a millennium ago.)

My point is that companies have legal departments for good reason, both preventive (keep us out of trouble) and contingent (get us out of trouble). With those charters, most legal departments are fiercely conservative, to the point that they wouldn't even advise opening the doors if that could be avoided. After all, if you allow customers in, bad things can happen that are impossible if they're not here at all.

Thus, lawyers are not exactly the apple of legal pursuits.

When you must deal with the legal department, do so with caution but also in harmony. The worst thing that can happen is a dozen attorneys, paid to be conservative and without much else to do, will focus solely on you and your project. Like the Internal Revenue Service and an audit, *once they take you on they will spend $50,000 to recover $5,000, because they must justify their efforts somehow.* So don't thumb your nose at them.

The worst part isn't so much fee changes, because it's someone else's budget. They're much more concerned about protection and contingencies, and those deliberations and negotiations can last months—often more months than your buyer is willing to wait, or more months than the issue will stay alive, or more months than you have available to feed your family.

There are several occasions where you'll be told the legal department must be involved:

- It is a rigid company policy.
- All vendors' proposals must be vetted.
- The buyer is uneasy signing the proposal without support.
- Your proposal is in legal terms.
- There are exceptions to corporate policy being requested.

I think you know where I'm going with this: Where you can avoid it, do so. Don't couch your proposal in legal terms ("third parties shall hold harmless") and get rid of the "boilerplate." We'll talk more about that in the next section. Let's focus here on when you really can't avoid it.

Ask your buyer what causes the attorneys to react poorly, or what they may require that's missing. Find out if there are examples of proposals successfully submitted and approved without delay. (Don't forget, you're about to write the proposal and already have conceptual agreement.)

Ask if there is a specific lawyer who will receive the proposal and whether it makes sense to give that person a call. If so, ask directly what you can do to make the job easier and to comply ahead of time. Talk through anything out of the ordinary (you don't have a separate contract, simply the proposal, for example). Note anything extra required: proof of your errors and omission insurance, proof of incorporation, possession of liability insurance, proof that you are a business within your country, nondisclosure forms, and so forth. Assemble these and provide them with the proposal to prevent delays.

Exchange personal contact information so that questions not involving internal issues can bypass the buyer and go directly to you, greatly reducing the time involved. Find out if the lawyer is working on a wide variety of cases and, if so, what your priority is. (I found out once that the attorney was leaving for a two-week vacation the next day and if the file wasn't forwarded that day for reassignment, it would sit on her desk for the two weeks she was away and the additional week it would take her to sort things out post-return!)

In a smaller firm, there may be a single general counsel and if the buyer is the owner there may be little needed other than a request to "make this happen." But in larger firms, there are scores of attorneys, not all expert in these kinds of consulting projects, many of whom may treat you and the proposal and just another vendor contract as if you're paving the parking lot or selling pencils.

The most serious problem, however, may be the fee basis. Lawyers are notoriously time-based, so they may insist on seeing your hourly rates. Don't comply with this. The point is that the buyer, whose budget is involved, is the one who is deciding about the investment and consequent value, and that's not within the purview of the legal department. (Ironically, it's usually HR people demanding hourly rates with the ferocity of a piranha, which is why you should stay out of that river.)

Prepare your buyers for this, because you can compromise on that one. If they "back your fee" into hours they estimate, it will come out as $2,500 an hour or some absurd number, which will cause the entire machine to read "tilt." They will not understand hourly based billing, but fortunately, that's not a burden anyone should place on them.

Prepare your buyer about that contingency.

Those are the best practices for dealing with the legal empire. The primary problem in delay, and that can be fatal—you don't have a signed agreement yet. It's far better to avoid this particular obstacle course, and fortunately you can do that if you're careful and agile. Toward that end, not that you've seen what may await you, I've assembled the following preventive actions.

How to Avoid the Legal Department

The ideal that you must have come to realize at this point is to avoid the legal beagles. Fortunately, there are steps that you can take and that have been effective for me about 98 percent of the time over 30 years. In fact, the only time I've been unsuccessful in avoiding the lawyers is when there is a tough corporate policy demanding it, and even then I've sometimes evaded the seemingly inevitable (see the case study earlier about the buyer who could write checks but not sign agreements).

The avoidance part is in your hands, and here are the basics:

1. Don't use your lawyer.

   In the next segment we will discuss when to consult with your own attorney *but never start from that corner.* If you use your attorney he or she will naturally be as conservative in your favor as the client's legal force would be on its turf, and you'll wind up with a transmogrified proposal that looks like a declaration of war on Lichtenstein. Your lawyers will be trying to protect you. Let me assure you that's not what will happen. They will sink the agreement just as assuredly as if you took a torpedo amidship. So don't make that call at the start.

2. Avoid "boilerplate."

I provide proposal examples online as part of this book's Appendix. These are meant to give you examples of the approach, just as the details earlier in the book have. They are templates. But you'll notice that they contain no legal phrases, *per se.* Nowhere does it say "third parties shall hold harmless" or "any disputes will be settled by courts in the state of North Dakota." Once you insert this stuff you might as well have placed a salami in your suitcase amid all those sniffing beagles at customs when you return from overseas. You're toast. (Well, you can't bring toast in, either, as I think about it.)

3. Make the proposal a continuation of the conversation.

The proposal, as we've established, is a *summation,* not an exploration or a negotiation. Keep your language conversational. You can see in my examples phrases such as "You will be accountable for . . ." and "I will be accountable for. . . ." It doesn't say "Accountabilities established and agreed, the violation of which constitute rupturing the terms herein. . . ." If you write in the same manner as you've spoken, there shouldn't be any tropism toward the legal library.

4. Forewarn your buyer.

After achieving conceptual agreement but before leaving the buyer's office, discuss the legal implications in this manner:

I've found that we can begin rapidly if you and I can do so on a handshake, but occasionally the legal department becomes involved. Is there a way we can avoid what is inevitably a significant delay?

The buyer might set you straight and say, "Oh, I work with legal all the time and if I say I need something back in 24 hours, I get it." That's great, then ask, "Is there anything that we've discussed to this point that might give them cause for pause, or any standard issues they tend to look askance at?"[1] Put a plan together that will try to avoid the legal quagmire, or at least expedite a path through it if it comes to that.

1. Don't include penalties.

I've always detested penalty clauses because they are inconsistent with a solid, trusting buyer relationship. They typically stipulate that interest will be added if fees are late beyond a certain point, or that extensions in the timing caused by the client's scheduling problems may result in additional fees. Once you insert these kinds of caveats, the buyer has little choice but to solicit a legal opinion. After all, it's the buyer's signature going on the document, and it's one thing to commit one's budget but another to commit the company to possible expenditures that can't be rationally avoided. (The buyer can't absolutely control accounts payable or some other department's cooperation in most cases.) Besides, if this is a trusting relationship, then you should trust the buyer to meet commitments without threats.

2. Provide reasonable assurances.

You have some strong leverage in the proposal in your favor, most particularly the terms of payment, which are minimally

50 percent on acceptance and might be 100 percent on acceptance minus a 10 percent discount. (Remember that some firms' rules call for the automatic acceptance of discounts.) With that kind of money being paid—probably unprecedented with prior consultants unless they've read my work—the client will rest better with some "protection" or quid pro quo. That's why I recommend statements in the proposal such as:

> *We guarantee the quality of our work and performance of the accountabilities listed above. If that quality is deemed insufficient, or accountabilities are not met, and we cannot correct the deficiency within a reasonable time period, we will refund all fees paid.*

That may seem too open an interpretation to you, but it's only an option for the buyer, it's already based on a trusting relationship, and you're not guaranteeing results (which would be unethical) but rather your standard of performance. This gives the buyer something to rely on in exchange for rather aggressive fees and terms. (I've had one client in 30 years, early in my career, ask for and get his fee back, because I overpromised and dealt with people whom I mistakenly thought would be committed to the work. My fault. Like being hanged in the morning, this marvelously focuses your attention.)

3. Be prepared to deal with issues about *you*.

I've actually been asked on rare occasion, "What happens if you die?"! (I've usually responded, "I don't know, but I do believe in heaven.") A buyer will sometimes raise an issue about a solo practice that wouldn't be asked of McKinsey & Co. Don't stammer and waver. You don't want the buyer to get a legal opinion. Mention that you're in great health, there are others who may cover for you as you would for them (the real issue is sickness and disability, not death), and that in the worst case you hold the client funds in escrow and they are easily accessed and returned. You may note the longevity of your company and the types of clients with whom you've dealt. You want this to be a casual conversation, not nine paragraphs of legal literature.

Now, what happens if, despite it all, you need to consult with your own lawyer?

Utilizing Your Own Attorney

There are attorneys and there are attorneys. I'll tell you right now who you do *not* want:

- Any family member.
- Anyone who's giving you a "break."
- Anyone who is just starting out.
- Anyone whose expertise is not in professional services and contract law.

That's probably insufficient. I was speaking to a group of consultants and one actually proclaimed, "My husband is an attorney, and he's assured me that I do not need to incorporate or carry malpractice insurance, both are wastes of money. What do you say to that?"

What I said was to get a new attorney and a new husband, but I doubt that she did either.

So the first thing I need to make absolutely clear is that the attorney who closed on your house for you, or did the title search, or wrote your wills, or represented you in an auto accident, is probably not the right person for this. His or her *firm* may be appropriate, if they have multiple attorneys in different practices, and it's always good to stay in one place if you can. But

I have attorneys for contract, trademark, estate planning, and litigation—all different people in two different firms.

Ideally, your attorney should be adept at both contract work and the working of personal services firms. Thus, a seasoned attorney who has a private practice with one or two others and specializes in this area would be ideal, but they are hard to find because, by definition, they can't specialize to that degree as independents and still make money (just as with consultants).

The time to consult your qualified attorney specifically about the proposal process is at these junctures:

- If you do not use my kind of template, but invent your own format and wording, you should pass it by your lawyer not to have it rewritten in legal terms but to ensure that you haven't inadvertently shot yourself in the foot. Remember that you don't have to accept all the attorney's suggestions, but you should responsibly be aware of any potential risks the attorney unearths. You may have accidentally implied that your proposal can be applied to other areas at no extra cost, for example.

- When the client comes back to you with legal questions or the client's own attorneys' wording in lieu of your own in the proposal or on a separate document. This is particularly important in terms of nondisclosure and/or noncompete clauses.

A nondisclosure agreement merely demands that you will not reveal proprietary client information to anyone else. It's reasonable and many clients request it, though the wording can vary widely. These are usually mandatory when requested, but innocuous.

A noncompete is far different. These agreements request that you refuse to work with organizations similar to the client—most likely, competitors—for varying periods of time. When you are asked to conform to this request, you should charge more in your proposal at every option level, *because the client is removing a portion of your market for which you deserve compensation.* Here you must ascertain the time frame, exactly which firms would be included (nothing vague, such as "anyone deemed to be a competitor"), and which of your services. You might charge a premium, for example, of $25,000 not to work with two competitors with a certain offering for a year, or $250,000 to never work with them in any area.

You'll need your attorney's advice to make any adjustments in the agreement, because the client's lawyers will have structured this to their maximum benefit and to your maximum detriment. And this is something that your buyer really can't help with.

Another critical area is "work product." Generally, you take out the intellectual property that you arrived with, the client keeps what was theirs to begin with, and you jointly own what was created during the project. However, the client will often demand that all "work product" created during the engagement be strictly theirs (so that it can't be used with competitors, a version of a noncompete), *and may even try to insist that they own your original intellectual property to apply as they wish.* This last provision would effectively make your client a competitor, if they offered, say, your strategy approach to a third party.

This is why you need a careful legal review and opinion on such matters. I've seen consultants essentially "frozen" out of a vibrant market and/or surrendered their intellectual property for what they thought was a nice project but which in actuality ruined them.

As a rule of thumb, whenever your client returns an amended or additional document to you with words not your own, run it by your attorney. You aren't compelled to follow the advice, but you should know all your options. I noted earlier that the 32 pages from the Federal Reserve attorneys didn't really change anything, but that's a rarity. Most of the time they are stacking the deck for the home team.

You'll also want to be sure that you're not getting into unnecessary arguments. When Hewlett-Packard, for example, requests a copy of in-force errors and omissions insurance, that's reasonable and you should simply comply. But when some other firms request that you make changes to your liability insurance coverage for the duration of your work with them, that's both unreasonable and unnecessary and you should know that you don't have to comply. In many cases, a legal department will try to obtain an advantage, knowing they won't press the issue if there is resistance, but there's nothing to lose in trying.

Therefore: Consult your attorney once with your proposal template just to make sure there are no glaring problems, but don't feel obligated to follow all of the advice. Consult your attorney whenever you receive a legal form, advisory, or request from the client's attorneys, even if it's by way of your buyer. Then you make the decision about what's reasonable and not (our next segment deals with compromise). Make sure that your attorney understands your type of business and your type of firm.

But be master of your own fate. Attorneys aren't adept in the consulting profession. In fact, almost all of them are still charging by the hour.

Effective and Ineffective Compromise

Compromise is something you can live with, not something you would die for.

There are times when irresistible forces meet immovable objects. When something "gives" in such circumstances, it usually means someone has won and someone else has lost. Not good in terms of acquiring clients!

Thus, I suggest that you prepare yourself for the negotiable and nonnegotiable. And for that we need a brief digression.

You and the client each have objectives for a project, some of which are mutual and some of which are partisan. That's all fine and well. You both want the project objectives to be met and successful, for example, but you might want to be paid in advance and the buyer might want to pay you at the conclusion. You're both merely looking out for what you perceive as your own best interests.

Such personal objectives fall into two categories: must and want.

A "must" has these characteristics:

- Mandatory for your success.
- Measurable, so you know it when you see it (or don't see it).
- Reasonable, in that you're not asking for the moon.

A "want" is a desirable outcome or expectation that, while appealing, isn't crucial to your success and without which having obtained success is still possible and reasonable.

In negotiating, you *never* want to compromise on a "must," which is why they are usually few and far between, but vital nonetheless. You can sacrifice "wants" but usually with some commensurate sacrifice or concession on the other party's part. These dynamics are obtained in conflict resolution, persuasion, negotiation, and so forth. And that's why they're important here.

One "must" that you never negotiate is your fee. Don't forget—we've established that the proposal *is not* a negotiating

---

Glossary

Objective: A result desired, either an improved condition and/or a minimized use of resources. Achieving the most possible with limited use of scarce resources is a highly desirable condition for objectives.

Must: An objective that is crucial for your success, without which you will have failed.

Want: A desire that you hope to achieve, but which you can fail to achieve but still be successful in the larger framework.

---

document or opportunity. So when is it appropriate to change fees, when you meet stiff resistance?

- The client simply chooses a lesser option. Option 3 may be attractive, but if there is simply no budget, well, that's why we have an Option 2.

- The client makes *quid pro quo* concessions. That is, *you remove value to justify the lowering of a fee.* This may mean that you don't include the international people or don't provide quarterly visits, and so on. (Most buyers love to try to reduce fees, but detest losing value, so this technique is highly effective.)

- There is an alternative offer of value to you. The client offers introductions to a trade association, which is chock full of your prospects, or offers to film an event for free, or offers bartered services that are attractive (don't forget that these are taxable).

So, to preserve fee integrity, never lower your fee on any option without one of the conditions above prevailing.

What you can negotiate and compromise on are your terms. That's why I recommend such maximally attractive terms for you at the outset: 50 percent in advance and 50 percent in 45 days, no matter what the duration of the project or its size. The client (and the attorneys) may react poorly to that, or they may have some problem with the overall fee and you can use this to mollify them.

You can always "retreat" to 25 percent on acceptance (that's not "commencement" but "acceptance"), 25 percent in 45 days and 25 percent in 90 days (assuming it's more than a three-month project). I would advise to never accept less than a 25 percent down payment, and never accept monthly payments (excluding retainers, and even there you should be paid quarterly at the beginning of the quarter). *Never, ever agree to payment "upon completion."* You'll find in those circumstances that things are never complete, and if your buyer changes or conditions change substantially, you'll never collect that final payment.

Keep your payments maximized toward the front end, starting heavily in your favor so that compromise is still quite good for you.

Be careful about compromise on timing. You don't want to have the project "hanging out there" and suddenly being requested when you're committed to three others. So explain when you're ready to begin under "timing" and when the client agrees to go forward to solidify the calendar start dates.

Feel free to compromise on the small stuff. You may have anticipated 20 people in certain groups, for instance, but if the client wants 30 don't look at it as a 50 percent increase, because you're billing based on value, not head count. If the client requests the following, be big about it:

- Extra debriefing days.
- Larger class enrollment.
- Additional copies of materials.
- Discussions with key subordinates or superiors.
- Your presence at certain internal meetings.

But don't agree to the following:

- Additional work beyond the proposal ("scope creep").
- Transfer of your intellectual property without compensation (e.g., in licensed form).
- Running more events (focus groups, meetings, and so on) than you deem are necessary for quality and communication.
- Presence at irrelevant gatherings (customer social events, unnecessary meals).

If you're prepared for what's in the realm of compromise and what isn't, you won't be caught suddenly saying "Of course" in response to a request that's going to seriously cost you. Never default to the position that if you don't do something you'll lose the project. There are worse things.

Like losing your shirt.

The Golden Handshake

The transactions discussed here are based on a strong and trusting relationship, so it's safe to make some assumptions based on the sequence shown in Figure 7.1.

Shared values about business (e.g., whether downsizing is proper, the role of outsourcing, honesty with investors) can lead to trusting relationships. On that basis, conceptual agreement about objectives, measures, and value is possible, after which a proposal with options can be submitted with high probabilities of acceptance. Once a project is implemented, the results serve to reinforce the original relationship.[2]

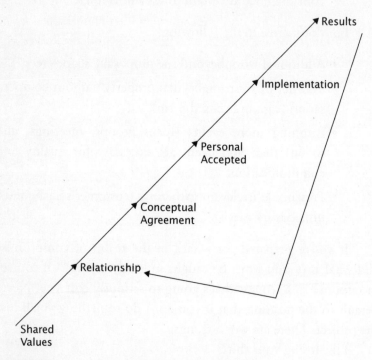

FIGURE 7.1 A simple business sequence

Succeeding steps are built on original trust and the increased trust that ensues from working together as partners and peers. *This is why I emphasize here (and in all of my work) that positioning yourself as a peer, partner, and trusted advisor is so critical to success.* Once your own demeanor, response, insecurity, language, and other factors place you in a subordinated position, as they say in Vegas at the craps tables, "all bets are off."

With that basis established, the "golden handshake" is the potential to begin a client based on the buyer's word and nothing more. That handshake may be physical, but it's just as likely to be by phone or even e-mail. I talked earlier about "pouring cement on the sale," meaning to show up as soon as possible after the proposal is accepted to demonstrate work has begun, and/or to do so even earlier. This is the result of the golden handshake.

When you have a trusting relationship and the buyer says something like, "It will take me a week to sign and return your proposal and generate a check, but there's an ideal opportunity this week to meet with my entire team in one place, can you do that?" it's time to spring into action. That's a highly responsive, reactive action that will help to "guarantee" the buyer's acceptance—you'll be on-site, visible, involved, representing your partner, and so forth. It's not impossible, but highly unlikely you'll be told that you can't go forward after that debut performance.

However, there are also proactive means to enforce the handshake. The buyer may say, "We're a 'go,' I just have to physically sign the documents when I return from London next week, but I wanted to alert you that we're accepting Option 2 and want you to put aside the time."

To which you should respond, "That's wonderful, why don't I begin some of the initial interviews now to hit the ground running? May I call your assistant and obtain some of the contact information, and let's you and I schedule a meeting for the day after you return."

In this case, you're suggesting the opening act, which is hard to say no to because it's basically noninvasive. Note the options. The buyer *could* say, "I need to talk to my people first, so hold off on the interviews, but let's schedule that day together." Or conversely, "I'll be submerged for a few days, but do start the interviews and let's schedule the meeting for a week later, when I can also give you the signed proposal and check." The more options you provide to begin, the more likely the handshake will be accepted.

In all of my experience, I've never had a contract reneged on or even changed once the buyer and I have agreed to initial actions even before the proposal is signed and a check generated. That's why I call this "golden." Pragmatically, you need to show up and begin.

Not only haven't I ever lost such work, but I've "saved" the contracts when intervening elements would have undone them. Natural disasters, deaths, terminations, competitive moves, market plunges, and other uncontrollable events would have at the least forestalled several of my contracts if I hadn't shown up and begun work.

You can't beat being present. This can taper off as your project moves forward and your labor intensity declines as planned, but it helps to be there early and often if you can, prior to the formalization of the contract. *The longer you wait for anything, the more bad things can happen.*

I've tried to illustrate in this chapter that it's wise to try to avoid the legal department altogether. That means not provoking the legal hornet's nest by poking it with your own lawyers and/or legalese. Once it becomes inevitable, work with them or your buyer to minimize concerns and conservative frenzy. Under certain conditions, do consult your own attorney, but ensure that the resource you use is well versed in your type of business and concerns.

You'll have to compromise at times, but if you are clear about and prepared to protect your individual "musts" and trade away "wants" (maintain the fee, change the terms slightly if you need to) you'll still have a great project and the client will feel that you've met halfway—even if it's really your side of the field.

Let's move now to a not uncommon but nonetheless dreadful aspect of proposals—when they're actually requested, which can be the worst thing in the world for your business interests.

Notes

1. These principles work well with procurement and accounts payable, as well. For example, with this question, the buyer might point out that payments cannot be made in two different fiscal years, and you'll want to know that at this point.

2. Which leads to more business and referral business, the "second sale" made at the time of the first sale. For a detailed explanation, see my book *Million Dollar Referrals* from McGraw-Hill (2011).

The Dreaded RFP (Request for Proposals)

Why Fill Out the Truly Boring in Triplicate?

The Beauties of Being a Sole-Source Provider

An RFP is a "request for proposal." It is most commonly used by government agencies, but you'll also find them applied in nonprofits and some for-profit entities. They are a blight on the crop.

These are usually issued by low-level people who have an arbitrary alternative in mind. They'll issue an RFP for a "two-day retreat for team building." And they'll have criteria that match the worst of the want ads: "The successful bidder will have 10 years of team-building experience with nonprofit arts groups." That experience may be desultory and with arts groups that collapsed—no matter. These are input-driven monstrosities. The questions will include such things as: "How many people will work on the project, will they commute or require travel, will they spend an entire day on-site, and will they eat bread crusts or cut them off if they dine in the cafeteria?"

Thankfully, there is hope. The FAR Act (Federal Acquisitions Regulation) states that even government purchasers in the United States may choose vendors based on value and not solely price (but you're still a vendor). But a great many agencies and other organizations still prize RFPs as a way to fairly evaluate suppliers. This may work for people who pave parking lots or sell plants for the hallways, but not, unfortunately, consultants.

The best way to circumvent RFPs and render them irrelevant is to be a "sole-source" provider. Such a provider is exempt from competitive requirements because of a uniqueness not found among competitors, rendering competitive proposals moot.

For example, Jim Collins wrote *Good to Great,* Michael Hammer wrote *Reengineering,* and I wrote *Million Dollar Consulting.* We are unique in having written those books and the attendant intellectual property. Hence, we are "sole sources" and may be hired directly by the interested party, despite rules for competitive

Case Study: The Navy and Me

Many RFPs are still in hard copy and require painstaking attention to the requirements. For about a year, the Navy sent me RFPs for a variety of projects. I ignored every one. It would have cost me more to try to compete for them than the project was worth.

Finally, the Navy sent me an inquiry. They wanted to know why I wasn't responding to their RFPs. And would I please fill out my response in triplicate and send it back!

proposals in other circumstances. This applies to books, intellectual property, models, experiences, accomplishments, and so forth. An organization can hire you directly if you can justify that you're the only one of your kind. That's surprisingly easy to do, and far superior to the RFP morass.

One of the advantages of developing intellectual property and writing commercially published books is that you can stand out in the crowd.

If you're approached by an organization that wants you to compete in the RFP process, your immediate position should be that you can be considered a sole-source alternative. Are you arranging your body of work to support such an assertion?

Figure 8.1 is a simple graphic.

It depicts a hiring and delivery of results process. There's nothing earthshaking, but if this were your property with appropriate supporting material you could make a case for sole source. It doesn't have to be elaborate or unprecedented. It just has to be

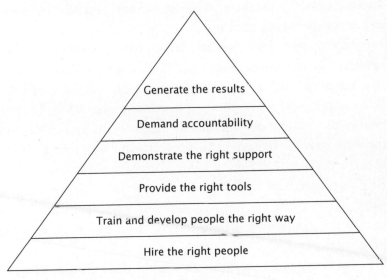

FIGURE 8.1   Sole-source material

yours in a configuration that's distinct and yours. Protection such as copyrights, service marks, trademarks, and registration further your claims.

RFPs can appear to be manna from the skies, offers that just descend on you. But they are mostly time wasters and chimeras. Even if you're successful in your bidding, you'll find that costs (fees) are fixed and unattractive.

My advice is to refrain from responding to most RFPs unless you can easily make the case that you are a sole-source provider and the prospect readily agrees to that. In the rest of this chapter, I outline how you can deal with these random events if you insist. But my warning early on is that these are tedious and futile endeavors unless you can put yourself in some advantageous position.

The worst part is that these RFPs are almost always generated by low-level people who use all the wrong criteria in evaluating the applicants. They are not buyers, and will merely cull the applicants to present a feasible group to the real buyer. There are no relationships possible, and the purchase might as well be made from a catalog.

Fortunately, these are rare. If you find yourself in a market where they predominate, such as state government, I'd find an alternative market. You simply can't gain sufficient or valuable enough business responding to conventional RFPs, because neither the volume nor the quality (high fee) is attainable. But there are ways to circumvent this process, and we'll take a look at them further on. Don't feel as if you're restricted to a conventional RFP response. If you can't prove that you're a sole-source provider, there are other options available. At least make the attempt to take these poor propositions to turn them into more valuable proposals.

I've never met anyone, in 25 years in this business, who has a viable and lucrative consulting practice based on a preponderance of RFPs. You can look at them as Really Foolish Positions.

How to Massage RFPs so That They Look Like You

Another method of dealing with RFPs is to make them into bespoke offerings! (I rarely get to use that wonderful word in a sentence!)

Some buyers will love you but they're forced to use a competitive bidding system because of strict organizational rules. In this case, have the buyer (not some lower level committee) "design" the RFP around you. Even if you don't qualify for "sole-source" purchasing, this is the equivalent.

The RFP in this case can list criteria such as:

- Worked for extended periods in London and Sydney, where our two major overseas offices are located.
- Speak Spanish, where our expansion plans are highest priority.
- Has coached at executive level in the pharmaceutical industry.

You get the idea. There will hardly be hundreds of people applying. That means that you can pretty much have the field to yourself.

This approach requires a tight relationship with the true buyer, and that is often much harder in RFP situations. We talk later in the chapter about how best to attempt this when you receive an RFP of interest, but let's talk here of the "front end," before it's even issued.

The entire point of market gravity is to create interest in your work among economic buyers and, once contacted, to ascertain who the economic buyer really is. If you're able to do that consistently through your speaking, publishing, networking, Internet activity, and so forth, you will meet buyers who can write a check immediately and others who must go through the competitive bidding process.

The good news is that the bidding process must be instigated by someone, and you've found that someone. So when the buyer explains (or complains about or bemoans) the need to create an RFP, suggest that perhaps you can recommend some important criteria based on what the buyer has explained about needs. (Many buyers don't need this hint, believe me.)

The two of you can then collaborate on getting you hired. In many cases, the buyer can even create work flow that will enable your value-based fees to be readily accepted (since RFPs are notoriously based on hourly and daily rates otherwise). Even if there are a few other consultants around with similar credentials and experiences, the odds are that:

- They aren't going to learn of this RFP.
- Even if a couple of consultants turn up, they don't have the relationship with the buyer that you've established.
- The odds are still better at one in three than one in a thousand.

You can see how much of an advantage you'll get from market gravity and bespoke RFPs than you would have in just responding to the ones figuratively marked "occupant" when they hit your company mailbox!

Some of the characteristics useful in helping the buyer "design" an RFP for you, in addition to the precise nature of the project:

- Language capability
- International experience
- Industry experience
- Professional (acknowledged) credentials[1]
- Publishing (articles, columns, assuming no commercial book)
- Education
- Experience running companies, sales forces, start-ups, and so on

Once you begin to combine several of these you've narrowed the field by leaps and bounds until it's almost the same as, "Get me James McGee." It can be that specific.

This approach to RFPs is what I call "preventive," because it focuses on dealing with them before they're issued. (So does sole source in most cases, because after an RFP is issued it seldom calls for "a book published on lean manufacturing in the construction industry" as a criterion—they are by definition more generic.) We talk about "contingent" approaches, what to do after you receive an RFP that is very generic, in the last part of this chapter.

The case I want to make here is that RFPs are a waste of time *only if you surrender to their terms and conditions, and the very nature of the beast.* If you prepare yourself to deal differently before and/or after, you can achieve success with these. It's not unusual for a series of RFPs over the years to be created just for you once you've done a great job with the initial project.

But you cannot take this particular preventive action with a committee, nonbuyers, or after the fact. Bespoke RFPs are possible only under these conditions:

- An economic buyer has come to you or you've reached one yourself, prior to any RFP being issued.
- You establish rapport and a trusting relationship with that buyer to the extent that the buyer is prepared to design an RFP that will enable you and few others to be considered.
- You suggest and possess the distinctive features that design the profile of the successful candidate.
- The basis is so clear and reasonable that even a screening committee would have no hesitation at passing your name on once you've complied with the RFP requirements for submission. That same committee will eliminate virtually everyone else.

To place things in perspective, I've succeeded with this approach on a handful of occasions before I became a true sole-source provider through my range of books and unique experiences. But during that period I was never successful on any RFP for which I merely complied with submission requirements, even though I may have been superbly well qualified for the project. I suspect that most of the problem was around my fees.

I offer this as an alternative, not a panacea, especially where you've met an interested buyer first who now needs to get you through the competitive bidding process.

How to Offer Additional Value

There are times when the best way to win the bid on an RFP is to offer even more value than the prospect requested.

Once you comply with the details requested in an RFP, always try to add additional value. The purchasers are not required in most cases to choose the lowest proposal, as if this is a highway paving project or a request for textbooks. They can identify and choose the highest value *that represents the greatest return for their investment.* That's where your creativity can turn the tide.

Here are factors to consider that are often either overlooked or considered implicit in an RFP that your competitors might not highlight or address:

- Preparation work.
- Surveys of employees, management, customers, suppliers.
- Tests of assumptions for validity.
- Reinforcement tools on the job.
- Monthly "boosters" via newsletter, special website, e-mail, and so on.

Case Study: *USA Today*

I had been contacted by someone I knew at the newspaper *USA Today* and asked to bid on an RFP. I agreed and did so, and was named one of the finalists, so I was invited to make a presentation to the inevitable committee.

About 30 people sat around a U-shaped conference table with the finalists, one by one escorted in and out as if they were Grand Jury witnesses in some organized crime ring, presenting their best arguments. I alternately felt like a criminal and a performing seal.

Yet my contact told me I had an "inside track" from what she had seen, and wanted me to throw all of my energy into this. I did, everyone asked questions and made notes, and I left and waited. And waited. Remember, the longer it takes, the more bad things happen.

Finally, I called my contact who sheepishly told me that another firm had been chosen. "Was I just too expensive?" I asked.

"No, the winners were more expensive than you," she confided.

Now I was stunned. "How could that be?"

"Well, they offered to also train the managers of the people going through the initiative to better reinforce the results on the job."

"But the RFP didn't request that!"

"That's why the committee liked it so much."

- "Audits" at fixed periods (quarterly) to assess progress and fine-tune.
- Post-project testing to compare to prior baselines for improvement.

- Compilations of best practices.
- Access to you for key people for given time periods.

You get the idea. None of these is especially labor-intensive or difficult, and most require no on-site presence at all, or only occasional visits. You can often derive these from reading the extensive background provided with most RFPs or through public meetings (see the following segment).

You can give options in your responses to RFPs, and I urge you to do so if you're going to pursue this route at all. The trick is to *ensure that your first, lowest fee option meets all the project's objectives.* Once you've established this, you can build on the value in your following options. You don't have to provide a "take it or leave it" or "make or break" proposal where the extra value you can provide is part of the basic package. This gives you two "shots" at the prize: The basic option for those evaluators who seek nothing more, and advanced options for those who would love to see additional value.

You never know what's going to constitute a "hot button." When providing "extra" value, focus on two conditions:

1. Something of a mild surprise to the evaluators. "Interesting, we never considered that, but it's a great idea," is the kind of response you're seeking here. That should set you apart from the competition.

2. Something in your own suite, so that it's easy for you to provide and not something that will erode your margin and keep you competitive.

Complete the RFP as you normally are requested to do, but use an "addendum" or extension to demonstrate your options and additional value being suggested.

I suggest one more opportunity to stand out in this crowd. It doesn't always work, but it rarely hurts, and you can use your own judgment: I often provide a copy of my own proposal format to accompany the RFP response.

I actually tell the evaluators[2] that, for their information and for the sake of comparison, I've also included a copy of my own proposal format for the project, which *in effect, can serve as an executive summary.* I like them to see the brevity and focus on objectives, measures, and value. And I like them to see the options in this context. It can often help you to stand out in a crowd.

One more key point before we move on: You'll usually have to "distill" the conceptual agreement on your own. That is, there is no trusting relationship with a buyer in the example I'm giving here, so you will have to "create" the objectives, measures, and value as you see fit from the information provided. The probability is that it's not presented in this manner, but rather as an arbitrary alternative, which has prompted the RFP. But the prompting occurred to produce *some results,* and you should infer what that is and work from there.

Even with an RFP, the evaluators are going to be better able to analyze your proposal and your worth if they can see their ROI, and the best way to do that is in *our* format, not *theirs.* So don't be bashful about creating your own objectives, measures, and value and creating the approach that puts you in the best light. There *are* objectives, they just have to be unearthed from the rubble and detritus of the RFP process!

So get your mining gear and get moving.

How to Use Public Meetings for Leverage

Most RFPs are accompanied by public meetings, at which prospective bidders can hear background and ask questions. They are almost never run by a decision maker, but rather by members of the committee responsible for issuing the RFP and vetting responses.

The meetings are very inconvenient, in that they may be held in the home base of the entity, say, Washington, DC, and you happen to be in San Francisco or London! However, there are often company or even governmental rules mandating such a meeting, so it's held. The assumption is also in place that large firms are going to respond, and large firms have offices in many cities and the capacity to put people on airplanes to attend the meeting. Occasionally, there is more than one meeting in more than one place.

You can let the issuers know that you can't attend the meeting and request copies of any handouts or a summary of any additional background provided. There may even be copies of visuals available. Sometimes you can obtain these items, sometimes not. You can also have someone else attend in your place, and they simply need to identify themselves as your representative, and not need to be an employee of your firm. This is a good reason to consider a colleague who is a member of a trade or professional association to which you belong, and a favor you can reciprocate in some manner. You can prepare this person with some questions, they can gather up materials, and provide insights on who else was there and what kinds of questions were asked.

If you can attend the meeting, I suggest that you arrive early and remain later. Talk to the organizers informally if it's permitted. Among the information you'd like to learn would be:

- How important is price and how important is value?
- What underlying needs prompted the alternative represented by the RFP?
- Who is the primary force behind the request (e.g., who is the real buyer)?
- What else is going on that has bearing on the request (what additional value might be powerful)?

- What has characterized winning bids in the past in this organization?
- What are the procedures after proposals have been received?

Also try to network with other attendees. Try to understand:

- What type of organizations are attending the meeting and might bid?
- Have they worked with this organization before?
- What are the distinctions of working with this organization?
- What is their usual process after receiving proposals?
- Are there likely to be further attempts at negotiation?

Listen to the questions asked in response to the information provided at the meeting, especially from those who have successfully bid in the past. These responses will give you some insights into the key buying considerations.

If you can establish any kind of relationship with any of the client's people, do so. There usually is no restriction on your contacting them at later points with questions or clarifications.

Here are seven techniques that may or may not be possible and allowed, but are worth pursuing if you are intent on bidding on such projects:

1. Find out who the actual buyer is and whether a personal meeting can be arranged.

2. Introduce yourself and do something to create an impression with as many of the committee members as possible, so that when they see your proposal they can relate to a name.

3. Find out about the "automatic rejection" issues, for example, failure to provide evidence of malpractice

insurance, or failure to provide a banking reference. Often, they don't ask you to resubmit, they simply eliminate you.

4. Find out the deadlines and time frames the group has in mind. There will be requests for your time needs, but if you can match them up to the general expectations of the committee, that will help.

5. Explore what other projects or initiatives are taking place, and their relationship to the one you're bidding on. You might be able to suggest synergies in your proposal.

6. Make sure that you learn the buyer's name and position, because you might want to try to bypass the process (especially if you discover that you just may be able to qualify for sole-source status).

7. Try to have a clear understanding through your formal and/or informal questioning as to what the preferences are that *aren't* stated in the RFP. These may include length, appendices, charts, staff resumes, testimonials, or lack thereof. Don't shoot yourself in the foot if you don't have to!

Public meetings can range from very informative to the dullest couple of hours in your life. They may be run by one low-level person, or by members of the committee issuing the RFP and, in rare cases, by the ultimate decision maker.

My advice is to avoid RFPs in general unless you can take advantage of some inside advantages, such as I described earlier in this chapter. But if you insist—or have no choice because you deal primarily with government or certain nonprofit entities—then attend those meetings that:

- Are reasonably inexpensive to attend.
- Demonstrate some advantage in your presence.

- Provide a unique insight or relationship that cannot be attained merely by securing the handouts.
- Represent RFPs that you feel you have a good chance for success.

It always helps to know "when to hold 'em and when to fold 'em," so I'd be doing you a disservice if I didn't make it clear when you should take your chips and walk away from the table.

When to Run for the Hills

This chapter on RFPs is about one-tenth of this book, and will probably be far less than that in most of your businesses and markets. I wanted to equip you with some of the top devices and approaches for maximizing your success should the proper circumstances present themselves.

However, I want to end this chapter with the advice that you will not grow a major business by responding to RFPs. There are firms that do this frequently and well, but they are very large, have other diverse income streams, or are highly specialized to work in government, institutional, nonprofit, and similar arenas. For solo practitioners these can at best be a peripheral and rare source of income; for boutique firms, perhaps a bit more. If you're not a sole-source provider, and can't have "bespoke" RFPs crafted for you, then this is not a propitious marketing endeavor.

Frequently, newer consultants will ask me about the viability and sustainability of a given market, such as education, or nonprofit, or government. I tell them that these are not pragmatic and high-potential choices. They argue back that they are passionate about them and:

- Know people making millions in that market.
- Can make it work.

- Would have the market to themselves.
- Are better than anyone else in the market.

Sorry, no cigar, not even close.

First, talk is cheap, and there aren't people making millions in those markets with the exception of some very large or highly specialized firms.

Second, passion is wonderful but not an anodyne. You can be passionate about flying, but flapping your arms and jumping off the garage will simply make you a public spectacle if you're lucky, and a corpse if you're not.

Third, having 100 percent of nothing is not valuable and you wouldn't have the entire market no matter what you think.

Fourth, I admire the high self-esteem.

People have long asked me how to make a lot of money. I tell them *not* to find a way to make a lot of money and try to become passionate about it, but rather to find something they're passionate about and try to make a fortune doing it. That may seem to contradict what I've written above, but it's highly consistent, in that what you're passionate about *also has to have a viable market and high-value need.* I'm passionate about exotic cars and electric trains, but I don't attempt to make my fortune by advising on either. These are *avocations, not occupations.*

Glossary

Avocation: A hobby or pastime that provides emotional gratification and that needn't provide income or career opportunity. Some avocations may lead to occupations.

Occupation: A person's usual work, job, or business that provides the financial sustenance to support a chosen lifestyle.

My point here is that RFPs are not likely to be able to sustain your occupation, in this case, consultant (or coach, facilitator, advisor, and so on). They are remote possibilities, which, on special occasions and/or at certain points in your career, may yield additional revenues and profits. They are not a fundamental marketing avenue nor source of income.

Run for the hills when you find:

- Your primary pipeline is "clogged" with RFPs.
- You are spending more than two hours a week on RFPs.
- You actually seek them out and place yourself on lists to receive them.
- Most of your delivery work is for RFPs.

Among the problems for you as an independent consultant or boutique firm owner are that even if you're successful in attaining these projects, the profit margins are inevitably thin. If you've made a mistake in calculation, or allow scope creep or scope seep to develop, *it's not uncommon to actually lose money when delivering RFP projects.*

You also will seldom receive referral work, which is the important second part of most sales when you close new business. You're working with low-level people, rarely meet a buyer, and the process is such that the only referrals you'll receive are to be on other RFP invitational lists, not for any direct business.

Although electronic submissions have negated the old "fill this out in triplicate" needs (in some, but not all cases, by the way), you'll still find these highly labor-intensive to complete, with a degree of detail almost unimaginable (e.g., what will occur in the morning session from 10 to noon; where will lunch be served; provide 12 references for whom you've performed this exact kind of work).

These projects invariably require—demand—that you specify exactly how much time you'll be on-site and someone—you can bet on this—will monitor these appearances. The labor intensity is severe. If you do not provide the agreed-upon number of days—even if all other metrics are being fulfilled—the client may ask for additional time or withhold some payments.

Payments are highly delayed. That includes initial payments, in-progress payments, and expense reimbursement. Forget about your dates, your amounts per payment, your terms. Not only will these be stipulated, but they'll often be abrogated by the client! You can complain all you like, but you have no buyer to provide clout and no leverage with anyone.

Projects can be delayed or even cancelled unilaterally. There is usually "boilerplate" language about this, but it doesn't matter. You'll be notified and expected to accept the decision.

I paint this dismal picture deliberately, because RFPs are situationally attractive, but not regularly beneficial. They're often the last resort of consultants who fear an empty pipeline or lack of business. But they actually can detract from marketing and business, and steal needed time from more pragmatic and profitable business alternatives.

You've been apprised. RFP: Really Finicky Prospects.

Notes

1. I'm talking about MBA and PhD, not an alphabet of honorifics bestowed by entities such as "coaching universities," which no buyer has ever heard of. Every time I see three or more initials I can't readily identify, I get suspicious about credentials.

2. Note that I refrain from saying "buyer" because you're really not dealing with one directly.

Retainers Are to Projects as Montrachet Is to Thunderbird

The Wonder of Access to Your Smarts

The Three Variables of a Retainer

A consulting retainer is vastly different from the typical "retainer" you might hear about from an attorney, just as Beethoven's Fifth Symphony inspires something other than the feelings you might derive from the hokey pokey.

Legal retainers are merely deposits, against which future hourly fees (in six-minute intervals) and expenses are deducted, right down to the cost of a stamp. But consulting retainers are payments that allow a client to have access to your "smarts."

> ### Glossary
>
> *Retainer:* A fee paid for a given time period allowing members of a client organization to access you as an advisor in a reactive mode.

Retainers are usually for a minimum term of a month, though I recommend a quarter (90 days) as the minimum (which I explain later in the chapter). They may involve one or a few people, but never dozens. They may involve frequent access or limited access or situational access. They are always *reactive*, in that the client calls you, you don't instigate the discussions. Think of being on retainer as being a mentor to the client, not a coach (the latter of which actively intervenes).

Retainers are "insurance policies" in some respects. They constitute a safety valve, or sounding board, or contingency for the client. People hope to never have to use their fire extinguishers, but they're comforted that they are present and that they work. You can find yourself providing one phone call a month and being held in extremely high esteem by your client. And always remember that you can maintain quite a few retainers concurrently, so that they are of high value and low labor intensity, the very definition of differentiated and successful consulting.

They also require a different type of proposal, because there is no discrete project involved, with a beginning, middle, end; there are not objectives, metrics, or value, *per se.*

Retainers are most common after a project or series of projects, because the client trusts you, you've performed as promised, the results are evident, and it makes sense to continue the relationship *even in the absence of a specific project.* Too many consultants simply disengage without having suggested a retainer to the client.

Think of yourself in an advisory role. Think of yourself as Yoda, from *Star Wars*! You're a wise person who doesn't assertively intervene, but who is there when needed, though probably somewhat less abstruse and metaphysical than the little guy. Presidents have had "kitchen cabinets," executives often use colleagues from their social and civic networks, and all of us usually have certain people we turn to when we need advice, even though we may otherwise not speak often. In police departments, they are often called "rabbis," and in business it's usually someone not in your direct hierarchical chain.

There are three elements that must be considered in a retainer relationship.

1. Who? (Number of people.)

It's important to specify in the retainer proposal how many people have access. The more people, the more valuable the proposal. It may be your buyer solely, or someone your buyer designates. Or it may be your buyer and three of the buyer's direct reports.

Retainers are never time- or activity-based, so it's important to keep this number small (e.g., six or fewer), and to reflect the value of allowing more people rather than fewer people. The criteria for "admitting" people would be:

- Who is vital to have access to your smarts for the buyer?
- Who will share the confidential nature of the discussions?
- Who deserves to be in a deliberately small group?

These people must be of the proper level and understanding that you're being accessed for advice, not for interaction in a project or for "hands-on" work.

2. How? (Scope of the retainer.)

The second variable is the nature of the interaction. For example, will it be strictly by phone and e-mail, or also by Skype, or sometimes in person and, if the latter, at scheduled intervals or ad hoc? A retainer is unlimited access—that is, without restriction as to number of interactions, but it can restrict the type of interactions.

For example, does the client have access during Eastern U.S. business hours, where you live, or also during Western business hours, where the client is headquartered? What about weekends and evenings? What is the response time—within three hours, or a day, or 48 hours? (My personal response time is generally 90 minutes during U.S. Eastern business hours, if we don't agree to exceptions.)

The more flexible you are, the more valuable.

If the client has a board meeting on the first Tuesday of every month, can the buyer access you on Monday evenings to review the next day's agenda?

Are you expected to meet in person (expenses would be separately billed) at given times. (It's fine to meet in person as long as the meeting remains simply advisory and not otherwise involved, e.g., conducting interviews, observing operations.)

3. When? (The term of the arrangement.)

As mentioned, I believe that a retainer must be in effect for a minimum of 90 days because it's too tough to see the benefits in a mere few weeks, since you're dependent on the client contacting you. Nor do you want monthly billing, which is too easy to simply abrogate at every hiccough that the client may suffer.

However, in 90 days, the likelihood is such that the client would have contacted you and found worth in the agreement. Remember, it's not the frequency but the comfort in knowing you are there as a trusted advisor, and the immediacy of your expertise and advice when a relevant issue arises, prompting the client to seek your help.

This basic Who/How/When approach is all you need to create a retainer proposal, a sample of which appears later in this chapter, quite different from a traditional proposal. It's unusual to begin with a new client in a retainer relationship (unless you have profound intellectual property and thought leadership), but it should be fairly common to create retainers with successful current and past clients, so you should become adept at these differing approaches to a highly lucrative business.

The Need to Control Scope Creep and Scope Seep

With a retainer, it can be financial suicide to allow it to expand beyond the limits of the three variables cited earlier. When the client does this, either inadvertently or advertently, it's known as "scope creep." When you do it by accident or out of guilt, it's called "scope seep" (a term I coined several years ago when I found consultants doing things that no one at all had ever asked them to do).

A retainer is a "fixed-fee" project with compensation rendered in consideration for access to your intelligence and judgment, but anything that enlarges its scope or size is a direct diminution of your bottom line. You must resist this at all costs.

Glossary

Scope creep: A project expanding and requiring more labor, beyond the original parameters set in the conceptual agreement and in the proposal, because the consultant is unable to deny a buyer (or even nonbuyer) who is requesting additional work. Generally based on feelings of inferiority.

Scope seep: Like scope creep, except initiated by the consultant out of guilt, lack of self-esteem, and other factors prompting the consultant to prove that he or she is "over-delivering." Generally based on feelings of inadequacy.

Ironically, scope seep is the worst and more frequent hazard. It usually occurs when the consultant feels that he or she has not been accessed "enough" by the client to justify the fee. So the consultant unilaterally offers one or more of the following additions:

- Extend the retainer beyond the current date at no additional fee.
- "Roll over" unused months to the future, sort of like cell phone roll-over minutes.
- Call and write the client offering unsolicited help and opinion.
- Ask for meetings.

This happens all the time, invariably from consultants who feel that they're not worth anything if not being used and not being used frequently, at that. There is nothing incumbent on you to proactively offer help, because the very nature of your retainer is *reactive* and in response to client request. The client is paying for the comfort of knowing that you're there if needed, not to need you every day. A great deal of this is poor business judgment, but some of it is also ego need—wanting to be wanted, which I'll call the "Brenda Lee Plea," trusting that a few of you will get that.

Scope creep can arise from any level of the organization, not just your buyer. When I worked with Hewlett-Packard employees, they were very concerned about "undocumented promises." They would sign a $2 million contract with a client, and assign a large team to implement it. But during the implementation, lower level client people would ask lower level HP people for additional help, "while you're here." The HP people didn't want to cause offense, so they tried to fulfill all such work or promised to do so. These "undocumented promises" wound up eroding the margins significantly because so much more time and delay were entailed.

The resolution was to simply provide this script to HP people: "Unfortunately, I'm not able to make any changes to work agreements, but I'll be happy to give this to my manager today for a decision." That drove the decision to people at HP who could comfortably say no (or evaluate whether some of these requests were actually important to the project implementation).

You are your own boss, assumedly, so referring this to the proper authorities shouldn't take long!

Don't allow "guilt" about not being used and having that money "in your pocket" drive you to scope seep. The buyer is an adult, and realizes that you're there to be accessed when he or she deems it necessary. However, not being called is not the same as not being appreciated. If you want unconditional love, get a dog. Otherwise don't seek pats on your head from your clients.

It *is* fine to suggest regular "check-in" contacts. These might occur:

- Prior to important buyer meetings with colleagues.
- At designated times (e.g., every second Monday morning).
- When certain events occur (e.g., monthly sales figures).

Although we've been discussing retainers as an evolution from successful project work, they can arise as the *original* interaction with a client, particularly if you have strong intellectual property, a commercially published book, a powerful referral from a peer, and so on.

Retainers seldom run for more than a year, often because of internal restrictions but more often because it's hard to make such long-term commitments. Let's turn, then, to how to ensure that retainers are renewed.

> ### Case Study: The Bank "Project"
>
> I was introduced to a buyer at a large New York bank
> by a woman who worked for him, whom he trusted,
> and who had been impressed by some of my published
> work. We met in his office, where he had stressed that
> he only had 45 minutes before an important meeting.
>
> At the 30-minute mark, I realized that we were having a
> great conversation, but there was nothing he apparently
> needed that I could supply, even though we agreed on
> many ideas and he was receptive to my "pushback"
> on some of their practices. As I watched the clock tick
> down to the end of the meeting, I was stunned that I
> couldn't come up with a next step.
>
> Then he said, "I'm sorry, I have to run. But this was
> great. Call me on Monday and we'll work something out
> for you."
>
> I was speechless. "Ah, work something out? Like what?"
>
> "Oh, I don't know, some kind of retainer where we
> can call on you. I'm not sure at the moment, but I do
> know we need more smart people around here, and
> access to your smarts makes sense."
>
> This is why I insist that you meet solely with true,
> economic buyers. They can do these things.

How to Assertively Pursue Renewals

Retainers should never be by the month, as explained earlier.
There simply is insufficient time to show your worth, because
the client may not need your advice monthly, especially the first
month, and monthly fees are too easy to simply stop.

Thus, quarterly is the minimum I suggest and six months to
a year are quite common. Multiyear deals are somewhat more difficult because of budgeting requirements and internal rules.

So the question becomes: How do you assure renewals at the conclusion of the term? Here are some of my suggestions:

1. Summarize the value over the period.

Nearing the end of the retainer period, summarize for the buyer the issues you were consulted about, your advice, and the outcome. These are virtual case studies: the situation, intervention, and resolution. The buyer may have become so accustomed to your help that the depth of the outcomes is forgotten or simply assumed. You know the Hollywood sequence:

- Who's Audrey Smith?
- Get me someone good to play the role.
- Get me that Audrey Smith who played the role.
- Get me Audrey Smith.
- Get me an Audrey Smith type.
- Get me a young Audrey Smith.
- Who's Audrey Smith?

Keep your worth in front of the buyer by summarizing progress, especially nearing the end of the retainer term.

2. Agree that the retainer can be favorably renewed in advance.

If you have a retainer running from January through June, offer the option of advising you of an intent to renew in May in return for a 10 percent reduction in the fee. However, if the buyer waits, say until May or later, then the full fee will be due again.

As cited earlier, many firms require that any discount be taken advantage of in projects that are undertaken. This offer provides a benefit for the buyer and a huge benefit to you.

3. Keep the client apprised of the ending date.

Many clients honestly lose track, don't renew, and then call you three weeks later for help, putting you in the awkward position of providing it possibly free, or having to ask for money before providing it.

Drop a note or mention during a phone call: "Just a reminder, our retainer arrangement will end on June 30, which is three weeks away."

4. Watch for critical activities.

The client will probably need your help more if there are critical activities approaching, such as new product introductions, reorganizations, new technology, and regulatory reviews. Tell your client: "I know that the regulators will be here during August and our agreement expires in June. Do you want to continue it to cover that next period, which you've said is always chaotic?"

5. Listen for the buyer to give you an opening.

The buyer may well say, "In September, we're going to have to talk more frequently about the divestiture," or "I'm going to need your help for the October board meeting." At these points you say, "Happy to work with you on it, should we talk about extending the term of the retainer to include that period?"

The more the buyer relies on you the more comfortable the relationship becomes, but that means that the buyer may not recognize that renewals are looming. Don't allow yourself to become a "friend," and feel uncomfortable asking for repeat business.

It's not the quantity of time—the amount of calls or e-mails or meetings that create value for the buyer in retainers, but the quality and impact of the advice, along with:

- Responsiveness: These clients deserve to be top priority for return calls and e-mail response, preferably within a couple of hours.
- Flexibility: You have to use your judgment to respond to client need. I once flew to Pittsburgh on a weekend to facilitate an emergency meeting for Calgon. It wasn't part of the deal, but it needed to be done.
- Accessibility: Your client should have your business, home, and cell phone numbers, as well as a private e-mail

---

Case Study: Calgon

I had been working on projects with Calgon and the president asked about the best way to work together for the next year, so I suggested a year's retainer at $10,000 per month, with payments quarterly, but with a $20,000 discount if $100,000 were paid on January 2. We also agreed that we would mutually evaluate renewing the arrangement under the same terms in November.

We did that for three years, until one November the president said, "Alan, we're not going to do the $100,000." I started to desperately review what I might have done wrong or how I may have become complacent.

Then he continued: "Make it $130,000, you've been more valuable than you think."

---

address. There are times when unusual circumstances dictate quick and direct contact.

- Prescription: Retainers are not good vehicles to try to gain some kind of consensus with the client and/or the client's colleagues, nor is it a time to play therapist and ask, "Well, how do *you* feel about that?" Give an opinion with clarity, rationale, and succinctly.

- Ego control: Don't become upset if the client doesn't heed your advice, or doesn't call during an important event, or tells you flat out something won't work. You're an advisor, not a Magic 8 Ball meant to be taken at face value all the time.

If you follow these guidelines and heed this advice, you'll find that your hard-won retainer will stand a far better chance of being renewed. Most consultants do not work with clients for more than a couple of years, at most. That's because they engage in purely project work, with no retainers.

How to Stimulate More Retainers

I've been stressing that retainers are more likely as a result of top-flight project work with existing clients, but they may also arise from direct business with a new client because you have a position of thought leadership, outstanding intellectual property, high visibility, commercially published books, and so on.

I've represented this in the Million Dollar Consulting® Accelerant Curve in Figure 9.1

You can see that a progression of work with clients can help speed them down the curve, from areas of low barrier to entry

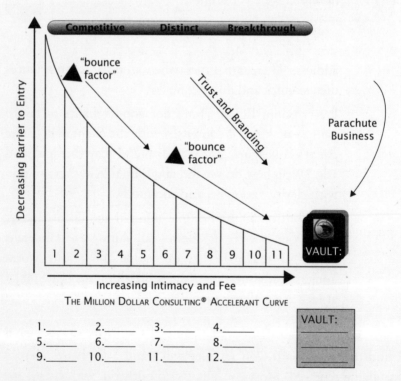

THE MILLION DOLLAR CONSULTING® ACCELERANT CURVE

1._____   2._____   3._____   4._____

5._____   6._____   7._____   8._____

9._____   10._____   11._____   12._____

VAULT:

FIGURE 9.1 The accelerant curve

(business with you), aided by "bounce factors" (e.g., models specially created for the client), that end up in your "vault," which comprises such things as licensing and retainers. Counterintuitively, perhaps, as fees increase and the intimacy of the relationship increases (bottom axis) *labor intensity decreases.*

That "vault" contains breakthrough work and singular value that only you can provide to certain clients. Although it attracts people who have come down the accelerant curve, it also attracts what I've chosen to call "parachute business," which is new business from nonclients, which can go directly to retainers.

If you observe people who are the acknowledged leaders in their field—Marshall Goldsmith in coaching, Jeff Gitomer in sales, Walt Mossberg in technology, Marcus Buckingham in personal development, me in solo consulting—you'll find that people are quite prepared to initiate a retainer relationship to have access to those respected "smarts."

Thus, achieving that type of "star status" no matter how small or grand your field will greatly encourage direct retainer business from new sources.

But what if you've not yet attained those heights?

Here are other ways to try to stimulate more retainers:

1. Let the prospects know the option is available.

Too often you're focused solely on your project work. If you look at the Accelerant Curve, you're featuring or speaking about only a few options in the middle. Make sure that your prospective buyers understand you offer retainers and the utility and value of them by:

- Stating in your casual conversation with prospects that "While I was on retainer with . . ." as a part of your language.
- Insert the same kind of statements in your formal speaking events, such as, "Here's why I love retainer work—I found myself being called at midnight. . . ."

- Write some white papers, newsletter articles, and blog postings that mention your retainer exploits.

2. Suggest it as an immediate option.

Remember the bank executive in the case study who told me he needs smart people hanging around? I was lucky he felt that way at the time. You should try to mention that there are several options for working together, one of which is a retainer.

3. Acquire specific testimonials.

Among your video and print testimonials should be clients who expressly mention the power of having you on retainer and how that relationship created tremendous value.

4. Use a retainer as an extension of value in proposals.

In your top option in the proposal, add a retainer to the project, with the hope that this aspect would be continued as a pure retainer in the future.

I thought this would be a good place to provide a sample proposal specifically for retainer work only.

Sample Retainer Proposal

Proposal for Marlin Perkins, CEO, the Acme Company

Situation Appraisal

You've asked me to serve as a resource on retainer to help in an advisory capacity by phone, e-mail, and an occasional meeting with your board preparation, retention issues, difficult customer situations, and related matters.

People Involved

I will be the sole resource from Summit Consulting Group, Inc. providing the responses and advice to you and your COO, Jim Perkins.

(continued)

Any additions to the two of you will require an amended proposal.

Scope

The two of you have unlimited access to me from 9 to 5 U.S. Central Time during the week by e-mail and phone. If not immediately available, I will return all phone calls within 90 minutes or, if at the end of the day, first thing the following morning. All e-mail will be responded to within 24 hours and usually much faster. We may have regularly scheduled calls at times we both agree on for whatever duration is needed. You may also contact me in emergency or critical situations beyond these provisions. Finally, we will personally meet if and when we both determine that such meetings would be critical to the resolution of high-priority company issues.

Any additions to this scope will require an amended proposal.

Duration and Timing

This proposal covers the 12-month period from March 1, 2012, to February 28, 2013. We will discuss an extension in December 2012 if warranted.

Terms and Conditions

The fee for this retainer is $10,000 per month, payable by quarters at the beginning of each 90-day period (e.g., $30,000 due March 1, 2012). It is noncancelable for any reason, including your not contacting me for given periods, and payments are to be made on all due dates as scheduled. The retainer may not be postponed, delayed, or otherwise rescheduled.

(continued)

We offer you a courtesy discount of 10 percent if the entire retainer is paid at commencement: $118,000 due on March 1, 2012.

Expenses will include only travel expenses should both be decided that a meeting is required, and will be billed as actually incurred. Expense reimbursement is due on presentation of our invoice.

Joint Accountabilities

Your accountabilities will include:

- Providing me with access to you and your COO, including personal contact information.
- Sharing financial details of costs of turnover, loss of customers, acquisition costs, and so forth, as needed.
- Responding quickly to my requests for information.
- Reasonable lead time when discussing urgent matters whenever possible.

My accountabilities will include:

- Signing nondisclosure and confidentiality documents.
- Responding to your questions and requests as stipulated above.

We both will be accountable for:

- Immediately informing the other of any new developments, which might materially affect the success of this project.*

*For example, the buyer finds out that divestiture is in the works, or I find out that three vice presidents have their resumes on the street.

Objectives, measures, and value are not included. You should include Joint Accountabilities as in our earlier example, and finally acceptance.

I don't allow postponements with retainers because you might be in a position of an eternal retainer in such a case. Here, you must hold fast to the agreed-on duration.

These retainer proposals are more like signed agreements—short, to the point, and easy. They simply stipulate the Who?/What?/When? dimensions and clarify that any alterations will result in an amended proposal.

Note that I don't usually include options here. My feeling is that a retainer is a retainer is a retainer, and providing differing durations or activities during it is simply distracting.

You may find yourself simultaneously delivering projects *during the retainer.* That's fine, it happens, and you simply create the traditional proposal for the project work (and there, of course, you can and should have options). But be careful: If you agree to a retainer and then agree to or suggest project work within it, you are going to lose your shirt as well as your house. There is no retainer large enough to cover the appropriate fees from the value of multiple projects.

So let me conclude this chapter by reemphasizing:

1. Project work involves a clear intervention, with a beginning, middle, and end, oriented to produce certain results, the value of which provide a dramatic return on your fee. You are the interventionist, even if you're using client resources, to ensure that the project moves forward. You actively intervene with as many client resources as are required for the objectives to be met. You are highly proactive with the client.

2. Retainer work is a relationship in which the buyer purchases the right to have access to your smarts under

limited conditions, which include people who have access, the degree of your responsiveness, and the duration of the arrangement. You are reactive to the client's needs. Almost all of the work is by phone and e-mail—remote.

If you keep these fundamental and significant differences in mind at all times, you'll have a great career—and submit successful proposals—for both project and retainer work with existing and new clients.

Finally, let's look at what to do when bad things happen to good proposals.

In the Unlikely Event You Need Oxygen

We Don't Anticipate a Crash, But There Are Some Things You Ought to Know

What to Do With Requests for Delays Based on Time and Money

There are times when the buyer will respond with the request for a delay. The requests are usually about time and money, in that it's not the right time, or there's another budget cycle approaching, or that there may be too much disruption at the moment. If you simply accept these requests in good faith, you will be doomed.

Here are my tricks of the trade for counteracting these not-infrequent requests:

1. Find out what's changed.

If nothing has changed, then the buyer wouldn't be asking for the delay. After all, you probably (should have) already asked if there were any obstacles not discussed after conceptual agreement but prior to writing the proposal.

So *something* had to have changed, *or* the buyer wasn't being candid with you before. Find out if it's a legitimate obstacle, such as a budget abruptly reduced or a new responsibility added, or if it's a chimera. If nothing has changed, then it's just an excuse.

If there is new information or concern, work with the buyer to overcome it. Any delay in your project will probably doom it. My estimation is that 90 percent of proposals that are delayed after submission are never accepted at all. Make these arguments:

- There is no time like the present. The project's advantages and value will be even more important in a tougher environment or with the threat of disruption.

- You've seen this before. You can adapt and you can help the buyer to adapt to the new circumstances as the project goes forward.

- The budget will be lost if it's not used. The buyer clearly had funds he or she was willing to invest. Those funds might well be removed or redirected if not invested in this project now.

- Offer to meet the buyer's boss if that would be helpful and is possible.

- Offer to reorient your efforts and the project to incorporate and/or address the new priority and new issues. You're a valued resource, the buyer has a new need, money has been allocated—you can get a running start.

2. Find out if it's an excuse.

The buyer will sometimes offer a lack of money or time as an excuse. Here is what might have transpired and what you can do about it:

- Subordinates have learned of the project and are terrified. In this case, tell the buyer that lower level people are always discomfited when there is a threat to the "nest," but that you'll be happy to place a few of them on a steering committee to give them formal input.

- Someone else has learned of the cost and has objected, without understanding the value or ROI. Offer to explain to the offended party or to provide the buyer with the language and rationale to handle the objective.

- As in my case study, your buyer may be "big hat, no cattle" and be intimidated about actually approving the work. In this case, don't throw good money after bad. Some people are just afraid.

3. There is a legitimate cause for pause.

The buyer may be undergoing a personal setback in terms of a family problem, illness, or finances; the organization may have added responsibilities to the buyer, demanding that the buyer travel somewhere, or actually frozen all budgets. These events happen all too often.

Try to establish the best time to pick up the discussion again. If the matter is personal and you know that, provide some breathing space and simply keep in touch with the buyer's assistants until you're told that things have stabilized and he or she is attending to work again. If it's organizational, work with the buyer to choose definitive review dates and times to assess next steps.

Legitimate delays aren't always fatal, though they are most of the time. Try to "stay in the game" with frequent contact and

Case Study: The Hospital CEO

I was introduced to the CEO of a major hospital group who needed coaching, because he wasn't getting along with a key subordinate and also had problems with his boss, the board chair. We agreed to meet in person, and he flew in on the company's private jet. I picked him up in my Bentley convertible, and he told me he had a similar model.

We spent two hours at my house and, as a result, I FedExed a proposal after taking him back to the airport and the private jet.

My top option was a $45,000-a-month coaching relationship, with less expensive Options 1 and 2. After a week, he finally returned my messages, and said that Option 3 was clearly the only one that made sense, but he could never justify the cost. He was afraid of what his disruptive subordinate might say to his prickly chairman of the board.

"But your jet trip to see me cost you that much," I pointed out.

"Yes, but no one really knows the purpose of that trip."

So the Bentley-driving, million-dollar CEO had to opt out because he was afraid of what others might think. Of course, he could have funded this himself, but that was apparently unthinkable. You can't win them all.

review of status. Remind the buyer that the terms in the proposal are not eternal, and that your availability and your fees may change abruptly.

But *most of all,* remember that time and money are *not* resources, but are rather priorities. So don't fall victim to a wait until resources are forthcoming. Instead, build a case that you and your project represent a larger priority than those to which money and time are currently being invested. This is what can dramatically shorten your process and best overcome this objection.

If you're a large enough priority, resources will flow to you nonetheless. Continually demonstrate your importance to your buyer, the organization, and the results that were specified in the proposal. All good things do not come to people who wait.

They come to people who make their case.

What to Do If Rejected

We all experience "defeat." The best hitters in baseball are successful only about a third of the time. The best soccer players might score once every other game. The important thing is to get up to bat and to be in the game. You can't hit if you don't swing, and you can't score if you're on the bench.

Moreover, success is a matter of small amounts. The horse that wins its race by a nose gets the same purse and prize it would have received if it had won by six lengths. First is first, it's not measured by degree. And that first place finish is worth about 10 times the prizes awarded to the second-place horse. But the winner didn't have to train 10 times as hard, have 10 times the investment, or run 10 times faster.

It just had to win by a nose.

On the golf tours, the first-place prize is often in the millions, and tends to dwarf the prizes for second through 10th places. But do you have any idea of the difference in strokes per round between the winner of tour events and the 10th-place finishers? How many strokes difference, per round, do you think it takes to be first rather than 10th?

Less than one stroke per round, that's how many.

My point is that there is a razor-thin line of demarcation between winning a proposal and it being rejected, and that you can turn things in your favor by following my system and processes to enhance your odds. (I'm actually writing this segment in Las Vegas at the Bellagio Resort, and the smart thing to do in the casino is to play games least in the house's favor and most in your favor. Blackjack is good, roulette is not.)

No matter how well we play the game, we sometimes lose. An unattributed quote that I particularly like:

You win some, you lose some, and some get rained out. But you have to suit up for them all.

So what happens when you're rejected? Here are the absolutely critical factors you need to consider to avoid thinking and acting as if it's a disaster:

1. Don't take it personally.

Let me put that another way: Don't take it personally! This isn't about you, or your worth, or your beliefs. Don't generalize from a specific, as in, "My proposal was rejected after all this work and time, I must not be cut out for this work." Use the points below to extract worth and value and improve.

2. Find out why.

Ask your buyer if he or she could help educate you so that you can improve in the future. Don't be defensive, and never accept, "Oh, it wasn't you and it was close, it could have gone either way," from someone trying not to hurt your feelings. That doesn't help your learning. Ask this critical question, "What is the one thing I could have done differently that might have resulted in my getting the project?" Find out if it's something you said, or didn't include, or misquoted, or failed to understand. Then make sure that doesn't happen again. If you find you're getting the same feedback after several failed proposals, then you're just not listening.

3. Ask for future consideration.

You've built a fine relationship and reached the "finals" of this event. Why throw all of this away just because you didn't win

> ## Case Study: Barbara's Timing
>
> I was mentoring Barbara, who sent me three proposals that had been rejected over the course of two months. Each had some common problems, such as insufficient expressed value and poor options to choose among.
>
> "What should I do?" she whined. "I just don't seem to be able to master this!"
>
> "I'd suggest you send me the proposal before you submit it, not after it is rejected."
>
> She did that, and closed her very next deal for $80,000. Never try to fix what you can prevent in the first place.

this particular race? Ask the buyer if he or she would consider you for similar work in the future. They may well be quite happy to do so.

4. Ask for permission to stay in touch.

Another way of extending the relationship is through periodic contact. (How else would Point 3 above really work?) So ask if it's agreeable to:

- Put them on your mailing or newsletter lists.

- Check in with them after the current project is under way. (Sometimes an alternative resource fails quickly, and the client has to scramble to recover the situation. You could serve as the "relief pitcher.")

- Have them consider you as a sounding board on occasion if they need some assistance from an objective source. (A little "free consulting" might get you back in the door.)

5. Ask for referrals.

This sounds completely crazy, I know, but I've discovered a fascinating dynamic: You've established a strong relationship with a buyer, who may feel a bit guilty in not selecting you. This request provides some expiation and atonement. The buyer will often say, "You'd be just right for a colleague in marketing," or, "I know they're looking for help in R&D, call Moe Adams. . . ." It can't hurt, and it often results in a high-quality lead.

All of these steps assume a solid and trusting relationship with an economic buyer who happened to choose another resource for the work. That means that your opportunity to ask these questions and suggest these actions will be successful, because phone calls will be returned (don't use e-mail, for the reasons we've discussed earlier—make this as personal as you can—and in person is best because the buyer will be even more eager to be conciliatory).

Learn from your defeats, it's what they study in West Point. If you're not failing, then you're not trying. But if you're making the same mistakes over and over, then you're on a treadmill to doom.

Hop off that track and land on your feet.

How to Improve Your Proposals Constantly

You'll learn from your victories and defeats what you can do better the next time. My proposals have become stronger, not by changing the format—which I've found to be consistently effective for my purposes—but from the content I insert into the template.

By way of both summary and best practices, here are 12 keys for continual improvement:

1. Ensure that you are talking only to an economic buyer.
2. Establish a trusting relationship, no matter how long that takes.[1]

3. Gain conceptual agreement on objectives—results to be achieved.

4. Gain conceptual agreement on metrics—progress indicators.

5. Gain conceptual agreement on value—impact of the results.

6. Review and ascertain if there are any obstacles to proceeding.

7. Create a proposal with options or increasing value and fee.

8. Ensure that you demonstrate an impressive ROI.

9. Get the proposal in front of the buyer quickly.

10. Establish definitive next steps, times, dates.

11. Follow up as agreed on to find buyer's decision.

12. Implement as rapidly as you can to "pour cement."

Like a golfer who has to perfect tee shots, bunker shots, putts, course management, and so forth, you need to improve in each area until you are unconsciously competent in each. If these are the 12 steps to proposal acceptance, and you can master each and handle objections at a point in the sequence, then your success ratio will probably be well above 80 percent.

You may need to adjust your proposals and their format in view of:

- RFPs
- Retainers
- Legal departments
- Client requests and requirements

One of the greatest "threats" is in proposals that have insufficient fees in terms of the value being offered.

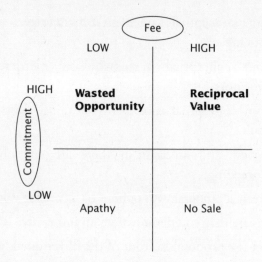

FIGURE 10.1   Fee and commitment relationship

When your fees are high and the buyer's commitment is low, you have no sale. When the buyer's commitment is low and your fees are low, you have apathy. When fees are low but commitment is high you have a wasted opportunity. Only when both commitment and fees are high do you create reciprocal value. (See Figure 10.1.)

The upper left shows where consultants frequently and habitually leave money on the table. They have a committed buyer and the potential to provide great value, but their fees are too low. That is money that is never recoverable. The entire point of the proposal process is to try to place yourself in a position of providing value in options that represent appropriate fees for the value in any given option.

You may find that in your markets your proposals need extra dimensions. Clients might want to know how many people will be used on the project. Or they might need to know who owns "work product." I wouldn't normally include such issues but I would be happy to include them for a particular client who has a good reason for asking.

When your proposals *are* rejected, make it a top priority to find out why. It's seldom the luck of the draw or the result of some committee. There's something you could have done a better job with, and it's usually involving the buyer. Too many consultants don't "run through the tape" but rather let up at the finish line. That is, they ask the buyer a few questions but not enough questions. They get information but not the most important information. They unearth some value but not the maximum value that the buyer would derive. There's a tendency to say, "Whew!" after the buyer answers a question that prompts the consultants to want to get it over with, rather than seeing an opportunity for further questioning and mining still more value.

The *format* is easy; it's the *content* that makes the difference.

Thus, the constant improvement of your proposals will be based on your ability to secure the highest possible content from your buyer. The time you spend in the buyer's office, asking questions and pursuing potential value, constitutes the most crucial aspect of creating a winning proposal.

How to Maximize Your Successes and Fees

There is an interesting phenomenon that accrues with success: The more successful you are, the more successful you become. Or as my father used to say from our lower class status watching those better off: "Them that has, gets."

As your proposals create high rates of acceptance, start to experiment with your approaches. After all, you're now playing with "house money." There is no time to try new things (and possibly fail in a good cause) as from a position of strength.

Some examples:

- Assess which options are usually selected. If it's usually Option 2, how can you make your Option 3 more compelling? If it's usually Option 3, then you may be charging enough for that alternative. If it's usually Option 1, then you might be putting far too much value in your first option, making the next two seem inappropriately expensive for too little additional value.

- Evaluate how many current and past clients have chosen a retainer option with you. If the number is only three to four per year, perhaps you're not aggressive enough in presenting the option. Or perhaps you haven't provided enough additional value for the buyer to want you to be around even after the current project is completed.

- Find out how many clients have chosen to pay the full fee in advance with the discount you're offering. If very few, then perhaps you haven't made the alternative sufficiently visible, or the discount is too small. If nearly everyone, perhaps the discount is too large.

- Assess how many of your proposals and the projects they represented led to repeat business and extended work (not retainers, but more projects). Investigate why this didn't happen even more often. Were you not providing sufficient ideas and incentives to continue with you, or did the buyer see you in too narrow a role, not suited for other things? Were you not meeting new buyers during your time on-site?

Let me dispel a myth at this point: It is entirely possible and, in fact, desirable, to market while you are delivering a project. The old rubric that "you can't deliver and market at the same time" is an excuse thrown up by people who don't know how to market!

> ## Case Study: My Surprise at Merck
>
> George was an international development manager at one of my largest clients, Merck, and he was my most significant single buyer, purchasing about $250,000 of consulting work per year through single proposals. He would take the 10 percent discount, and pay me $225,000 in early January, because Merck was on a calendar year as their fiscal year.
>
> I was asking my buyers at the time why they chose the discount so that I could determine if I was at the right rate or not. When I got to George, I received quite a shock.
>
> "Oh, I don't care about the size of the discount, or the discount at all," he said, smiling. "I pay your full fee in advance because that way no one can cancel my project."
>
> Talk about how stupid I was two weeks ago! It was in George's self-interest to pay me early because the inevitable "tremors" with a large company caused budgets to shift, but you can't shift a budget that's already been spent!
>
> I immediately added this to my list of reasons to pay me in advance—it's in *your* self-interest!

While you're on-site, you'll find ample opportunity to meet colleagues of the buyer who are buyers themselves. You'll also meet lower level people who would gladly introduce you to their boss. There is nothing illegal, immoral, or unethical about meeting these people and investigating whether a relationship is possible.

Your mind set has to be: I have tremendous value to provide, and I'd be remiss if I didn't offer it to these other people as long as I'm here.

The worst thing that happens is that nothing happens. But the criminal thing that happens is that you don't even try. I'm not advocating that you visit the client each day with PowerPoint slides and order forms. But I am urging you to seek out and create relationships with additional buyers, which I call "lateral marketing."

Quite a few of the people I've mentored and helped with proposals have been told by their clients that the proposal they submitted "made all the difference" at selection time. They've entrepreneurially suggested that perhaps their clients' own sales forces would benefit from adapting similar aspects in their own approach to customers. So in many cases, they've turned the proposal itself into an item of value for the client with appropriate compensation.

The overall format can be readily adjusted for nonmonetary purposes that still represent success for you in other areas. The sequence of establishing trusting relationships and identifying objectives, measures, value, and joint accountabilities is useful in gaining influence, persuading others, and creating consensus. The approach is useful on boards, committees, task forces, and so forth. The person applying the approach will usually be seen as at least the informal leader.

Options, of course, are applicable across a wide range of business and personal issues, and help to create compromise, defuse hostility, and move others from "Should I?" to "*How* should I?" You can provide your kids with alternatives, or your boss, or your significant other, or yourself. You can ask others to provide additional options to gain further inclusion.

The main consideration, perhaps, is to continually examine your fees. As your acceptance rates increase, place upward pressure on your fees (no one else will do this for you). You're always better off with a few high-priced proposals than a plethora of low-priced ones, even if the eventual total dollars are the same.

The client is concerned about value. Provide all the value you can, so that you needn't be concerned about fee, because the client sees huge ROI.

When to Stop Writing Proposals

Never, assuming you continue to work in professional services.

But there are times when proposal writing is far less important or actually dysfunctional.

For example, there are many types of work you can choose to do on a "handshake" or brief e-mail exchange after you're successful, well known, and have long-term relationships with buyers. Sometimes a proposal becomes "overkill" or even insulting to long-term buyers.

Here are five occasions when you can stop writing certain kinds of proposals.

1. When the project is very short term. In this case the buyer wants you to come in for a day to brief some key people on how best to deal with a hostile client, or to provide a day of coaching for a key executive. Just cite a price and do it.

2. When the project is identical to one in the recent past. For example, conduct a strategy review for Unit B the same way you did for Unit A about a month ago.

3. When it's a discrete task or deliverable: Provide a template for the steps all of our managers must adhere to in order to legally and ethically terminate a management-level employee.

4. Almost all retainers.

5. Singular "assignment events," such as speaking for a half-day as a part of a conference.

In these and related assignments you'd actually be shooting yourself in the foot if you subjected yourself and your buyer to the rigor of a full-blown proposal. A real or verbal handshake is usually fine in these instances. You can always document whatever you need to in a simple letter or e-mail.

Ironically, you *should* create proposals for most *pro bono* work, because you want a record of what was agreed on to prevent scope creep in a situation where you're not getting paid to begin with, and you want documentation of your success because a testimonial and references are going to be your key dividends.

Remember that buyers change and conditions change, and no handshake will trump a changed board policy or the transfer and replacement of your buyer. We've talked about the utility of accompanying a dreadful RFP with your own proposal.

I continue to use my proposal template today for all major client work and all major coaching work. As a rule of thumb, *any* potential project involving more than $35,000 or so should have a written proposal. Both you and the client deserve that protection. Remember that one of the benefits of a proposal that we spoke of early in the book is that neither party can unilaterally change it. Thus, this is a fundamental good-faith agreement between you and your buyer in a trusting relationship, which no legal team should be able to tear asunder.

The size of the proposal's project and its scope are not relevant to the size of the proposal itself—about 2.5 pages—so this simple document will ensure success and protect you while requiring very little labor investment to create and to track.

In summarizing this book, I'd like you to always bear in mind that if you leave $100,000 on the table each year—that could be as little as four proposals undercharged by $25,0000 each—you will lose $100,000 *that will never, ever be recovered.* That's a million dollars in 10 years, total profit less taxes, that you'll never see again. If you're leaving more than $100,000 on the table and/or for more years, you could easily be losing millions of dollars that are vital to your family, life, and business.

I've heard from thousands of people who read my former book on the subject that they couldn't believe that they "almost immediately gained $45,000 per proposal," or "raised the hit rate to 85 percent from under 50 percent," or "reduced time on each project by at least a third." These methodical proposals can save you time and make you money. Ignore them at your own peril.

Above all, this is a relationship business, grounded on the trust generated between you and your economic buyer. Don't be distracted. What's your value, who can write a check for it, and how do you find or attract those buyers?

You do that consistently and you'll provide great value to your clients and continuing wealth for yourself and your loved ones. Don't stray from that path.

That's my proposal to you.

Note

1. Within reason—several meetings are reasonable, but two years is not.

Virtual Appendix

We're featuring an online Appendix that is periodically updated with my latest intellectual property. Please visit my website, www .summitconsulting.com, click on "store," and then scroll to this book. You'll find a link there to the Appendix. Thanks!

Typical Approach

Proposals can vary a great deal, and we've provided examples that cover the range from formal contracts to informal letters of agreement. However, all were based upon previously-established conceptual agreement, and all provide a single fee for the project (or for each choice of yeses).

The normal framework for the value pricing proposal should encompass this basic sequence:

Situation Appraisal: Summarize and reconfirm the conceptual agreement concerning the condition to be improved and the desired state.

Objectives: The outcomes expected, both tangible and intangible, quantifiable and non-quantifiable. These should be expressed in terms of impact on the client's business, and sometimes are expressed again in the "values" category, if used.

Value: Either clearly stated or implied through buyer conversations, what is the value of achieving the objectives. This sometimes appears in the "objectives" category.

Metrics: How will the client evaluate success? What are the indicators that the objectives have been met? Simply stated: How would clients know it if they fell over it?

Timing: Projects are finite. When do we begin, when do we end, and are there progress measures in between?

Accountabilities: What is the client expected to provide (documents, access, administrative support) and what do we provide (focus group facilitation, product, reports)? What is the nature of the collaboration?

Credentials (optional): Why is Zenger Miller (and you) the best alternative for this client? This is usually already covered during the relationship-building. Sometimes this area includes the credentials of the individuals who will work on the project.

Terms and Conditions: What is the fee (including the options) for the project, how is it to be paid and under what conditions? How are expenses to be reimbursed, and what is included and excluded?

Acceptance: The sign-off by the economic buyer.

The following samples don't rigidly adhere to this format, but all of the elements have been agreed upon either implicitly or explicitly. They range from the short-term and relatively low-priced, to the extended, relatively high-priced. Some are pure consulting interventions, other include deliverables. None is meant to be "perfect." Use them as templates to guide you in creating value-rich, high fee proposals for your clients.

Note that tasks are rarely specified in detail. The "what" and the outcome are important. The "how" and the input are up to the experts—the consultants. If the project is value-priced correctly, the margins will more than support unanticipated client requests.

Sample Proposal #1

Proposal to Assist in Reorganization at XXXXX

Situation Summary

You must "jump start" people so that a new manner of working cross-functionally—in a matrix organization—is not merely accepted, but is exploited as a high-productivity way of life. Although reorganization has not been the norm, there is likely to be resistance, both from those inside and from those outside the new organization. A key factor—perhaps *the* key factor in success—is the ownership and appropriate behaviors of all key managers and exemplars, so that people have the proper leadership, and accountabilities will be accepted.

The primary transition is from a project-oriented, transient approach, to a program-oriented permanent approach in managing the business. Standards, measurement, tracking, feedback loops and ultimate ownership must be created and embraced. The *process* of ownership is central to success. Collaboration in a matrix structure with accountability thrust downward are important goals.

Objectives

Among the results to be achieved are these key objectives:

- Managers' skills are developed and behaviors are directed toward achieving and exploiting results that the new organization affords.
- Accountabilities are clear at the individual job (micro) level.
- Communications flow is rationalized so that people are able to deal within the "matrix" clearly, easily and willingly.
- Key exemplars develop and exhibit collegiality that demonstrates support for and participation in the new organization.
- Group interactions are facilitated and continually honed.

- Obstacles presented by systems, procedures and culture are identified and removed as appropriate.

Methodology/Interventions

The assistance in achieving the objectives would include, but not be limited to, the following activities:

- One-on-one assistance for all key managers in skills and behaviors required by the new organizational relationships.
- Group facilitation where needed in meetings and cross-functional teams.
- Group observation and feedback, with recommendations on how to improve the process.
- Assistance with written communications and meetings, so as to maximize ownership and accountabilities and minimize resistance.
- Recommendations for procedures, cultural norms (i.e., meeting types and durations) which will remove obstacles and strengthen the matrix structure.
- Assistance in creating ownership that encompasses standards, measures of success, monitoring means and feedback to those accountable.
- Observation and recommendations for interactions with "non-matrix" groups whose adherence to the new system is key to overall success.
- Attendance at large (off site) and small (on site) meetings to provide feedback on acceptance and recommendations on follow-up actions.

Measures of Success

We'll know we're successful when the following are manifest:

- New programs are introduced in a synergistic fashion.

- Other XXXXXX functions accept and utilize the new structure.

- People are focused beyond merely getting something working toward getting it working to a degree previously designated which constitutes success. (It's not just running, it's running the way it should be running.)

- There is group approval, and a lack of cynicism; the programs show multiple sign-offs from diverse team members.

- Meetings and discussions clearly reveal that others were included—and valued—in the decision making process, and that such inclusion was mandatory for success.

Timing

I'm available to begin working with you this month and, at the moment, the February 23 meeting date is one I can make. I'd suggest a 90-day initial phase, after which we'd evaluate progress in light of the above and make an assessment as to what further assistance is necessary. Our initial project would therefore begin now and last until April 15.

Joint Accountabilities

I would work with Cheryl (and anyone else designated) in conjunction with the project so that the interventions I'm involved in could be transferred entirely to internal people, if desired. We would jointly make determinations during the initial 90 days as to whether some of the objectives and interventions required more emphasis than others, and/or whether new needs arose that were unanticipated. In that case, we would redirect our efforts accordingly.

Terms and Conditions

My fees are always based upon the project, and never upon time units. That way you're encouraged to call upon me without worrying about a meter running, and I'm free to suggest additional areas of focus without concern about increasing your investment.

The fee for the assistance detailed above would be $15,000 per month, payable on the 15th of February, March and April. If you choose to pay the entire amount at the outset, I'm happy to provide a 10% reduction in the total fee. Expenses are billed as actually accrued at the conclusion of each month, and are payable upon receipt of our statement.

At the end of the 90 days we would make a joint evaluation as to whether to continue the relationship and, if so, under what conditions.

Acceptance

Your signature below indicates acceptance of this proposal and its terms.

This proposal is accepted and forms an agreement between XXXXXXXXXX (you) and Summit Consulting Group, Inc. (we/us/I) as represented by Alan Weiss.

For Summit Consulting Group, Inc.:   For XXXXXXXXXX:

Alan Weiss

President   _____

Date: January 31, 2011   Date:_____

Sample Proposal #2

Proposal: XXXXXXXXXX XXXXXXX—Performance Appraisal Skills Building

This constitutes a proposal tendered by Summit Consulting Group, Inc. to assist XXXXXXXXXX XXXXXXX, Inc. in the research, design, implementation and refinement of a performance evaluation process which is understood, supported, and effectively executed by designated members of management.

Objectives

The objectives for the project include:

- XXX management will possess the knowledge to execute performance reviews
- XXX management will possess the skills to execute those reviews
- Reviews will be conducted in conformance with company guidelines
- Reviews will provide useful and honest feedback to performers
- Performance improvement will be detailed and monitored

In achieving these objectives, the following parameters will be met in establishing and implementing the processes:

- alignment between individual and organizational goals
- linking tasks to output; that is, focusing on and measuring results
- seeking competitive advantage; the process must enhance business goals

- creation of a dialogue between performer and manager
- participation by and commitment from the performer and the manager
- simplicity of administration and avoidance of bureaucracy
- metrics for a *process* and not an *event*; follow-through and support
- combine skills and behaviors in the development focus
- global applicability, allowing for local cultural variations, as appropriate
- minimize disruption in implementation of and training for the process

Measurement

The success in meeting the objectives would be measured by factors which include:

- Creation of developmental plans for all employees evaluated
- Improvement in performance measures during the year following the first review period[1]
- Evaluations are performed and submitted by deadlines
- Minimum of grievances/reviews requested over disagreements in evaluations
- Random sampling of population indicates acceptable frequencies of monthly and/or quarterly feedback sessions during the year
- Minimum returned and/or "overruled" evaluations by senior management

---

[1]Note that this need not be represented by increased *ratings*, since the goal is to improve relative to current performance, and forced-distributions may still be applied.

Methodology

Option 1: Skills Building for Managers

We would work with you to research and design a classroom intervention which could be delivered by our staff acting as facilitators and by your own people as internal instructors. This option would entail:

- Investigation of the types of jobs and performance currently required by XXX and those jobs and performance anticipated by XXX.
- Assessment of current managerial competence/success/ failures in contemporary performance evaluation efforts.
- Incorporation of XXX business and strategic goals so that performance and assessment are aligned with organizational need.
- Creation of a one-day program, including concepts, exercises, XXX examples and support ("take-away") materials which would include:
  - how to coach and counsel
  - how to provide informal feedback on a regular basis
  - how to create performance objectives (behavioral and outcomes)
  - how to create measurement criteria
  - how to create developmental plans
  - how to engage the performer as "owner" of the process
- Creation of a "train-the-trainer" workshop of 2–3 days' duration, in which XXX people would be trained to conduct the one-day sessions.
- Creation of appropriate reference material and job aids for both sessions.

- Facilitation of sessions, as requested.
- Monitoring of results over ensuing six months and refinements as necessary as process is implemented.

Option 2: Skills Building for Remote Locations (Optional)

We would create a set of self-paced, objective-based (criterion-referenced instruction) materials to be provided in those cases when:

- Remote locations preclude classroom interventions.
- Small numbers of people preclude classroom intervention.
- Language difficulties require varying speed of learning.
- Refresher capability is required to update skills.
- New promotions or new hires cannot be accommodated in classes rapidly.

In this case, we would adapt the option 1 program into a set of print and video materials which contain their own criteria for successful completion, and can be validated by an off-site party, if desired. We estimate that this program would require from 16 to 24 hours to complete, and would be completely modularized. (We generally recommend half-day exposures.)

Option 3: Skills Building for All Employees in Performance Appraisal (Optional)

There is an opportunity to expose all employees (not just managers conducting reviews) to the need for two-party commitment to the process and ownership of it. By exposing performers to the basics covered in option 1, they are empowered to participate with a commensurate set of skills, and not be reliant on the reviewer and his or her prior training.

We recommend a three-hour session which fulfills the following:

- Employees are able to understand and question the process

- Employees understand their accountabilities and role in the process

- Exercises are provided in objective setting and measurement criteria

- "Receiving feedback" skills are developed (people respond best when they know *how to be coached*)

These sessions can provide for an equal dialogue between manager and performer, and increase the frequency of feedback since the employee understands the need and his or her accountability in asking for feedback.

Option 4: Integration with the Performance System (Optional)

As a part of our research and design activities, we can "extend our reach" somewhat and recommend and design the best ways in which to integrate the performance evaluation process into areas such as:

- compensation and incentive rewards

- developmental plans, training programs, and career development

- identification of high potential people

- succession planning

- recruitment

- performance improvement/probation/remedial/termination needs

- culture and morale issues

Since the performance system seldom operates in isolated parts, but rather in a dynamic interaction, the improvement of the performance evaluation process can serve as a catalyst to enhance the other aspects of the performance system. This is a relatively straightforward undertaking when we are engaged in option 1 and asked to examine the interrelationships concurrently.

Timing

Option 1: Implementation by June 30, 2011

Option 2: Implementation by September 1, 2011

Option 3: Implementation by June 1, 2011

Option 4: Implementation by September 1, 2011

Resource Commitments

Summit Consulting Group, Inc. will provide Alan Weiss, Ph.D. as the project leader. He will be continually involved in all aspects of the project, and serve as primary interface with XXX management. Summit's credentials have been provided in previous materials. We will sign non-disclosure agreements as requested, and all work in this project becomes the sole property of XXX. All of our work is conducted within strict bounds of confidentiality.

We will also provide all materials, audio/visual aids, computer work and other support services as required. We will provide masters of the final, approved materials for ownership and reproduction by XXX.

XXX will provide us with reasonable access to key management people, documentation and company information, as appropriate, within the time-frames outlined. XXX will be responsible for all scheduling of classes, facilities, equipment, and related support for training and development purposes. XXX will also adhere to the fee structure and reimbursement procedures outlined below. XXX professionals will assist in some data gathering, development of relevant examples and critique of materials.

Note: Facilitation of programs will be billable at rates shown under "terms."

Terms and Conditions

We assess a single project fee for our work, so that there is never a "meter running," and you can control expenses tightly. Within the objectives and parameters described above, we will commit as much time as necessary to fulfill the objectives and meet the time-frames. You and we may request additional time be spent on aspects of this project without any additional fees or charges, except for travel expenses.

Our fees for the options above are:

Option 1: Skills building for managers: $68,000

Option 2: Self-paced study for managers:
   print materials only 24,000
   print materials and video 46,000

Option 3: Skills building for employees: 12,000

Option 4: Integration into performance system: 18,000

Facilitation by our staff, any option: $3,500 per day, U.S., $5,000 non-U.S.

Training-the-trainer facilitation: included in the fee for option 1.

Payment terms:

Full payment of $68,000 at acceptance in return for reduced fee structure.

Further payment alternatives:

We will honor the fees for the optional methodologies through calendar 2013.

Reasonable travel and living expenses are submitted monthly as actually incurred, and payment is due upon presentation of our invoice. There are no charges for fax, phone, postage, duplication, etc.

This project is non-cancelable, and agreed-upon payment terms are due as described. However, you may postpone or delay any part of the work in progress without penalty. In addition, our work is guaranteed. If we do not meet your objectives, and cannot meet them after your notification and an attempt to correct the shortcoming, we will refund your full fee. This has been our commitment to our clients for over a decade.

Acceptance

This proposal is accepted and forms an agreement between XXXXXXXXXX XXXXXXX, Inc. (you/XXX) and Summit Consulting Group, Inc. (we/us).

For Summit Consulting Group, Inc.:   For XXXXXXX, Inc.:

Alan Weiss   _____

President   _____

December 6, 2010   Date:_____

Index